Philosophy of Care

Philosophy of Care

Boris Groys

VERSO
London • New York

First published by Verso 2022

1 3 5 7 9 10 8 6 4 2

Verso
UK: 6 Meard Street, London W1F 0EG
US: 20 Jay Street, Suite 1010, Brooklyn, NY 11201
versobooks.com

Verso is the imprint of New Left Books

ISBN-13: 978-1-83976-492-9
ISBN-13: 978-1-83976-494-3 (UK EBK)
ISBN-13: 978-1-83976-495-0 (US EBK)

British Library Cataloguing in Publication Data
A catalogue record for this book is available from the British Library

Library of Congress Cataloging-in-Publication Data
Names: Groĭs, Boris, author.
Title: Philosophy of care / Boris Groys.
Description: London ; New York : Verso, 2022. | Includes bibliographical references and index.
Identifiers: LCCN 2021041763 (print) | LCCN 2021041764 (ebook) | ISBN 9781839764929 | ISBN 9781839764943 (UK ebk) | ISBN 9781839764950 (US ebk)
Subjects: LCSH: Caring.
Classification: LCC BJ1475 .G765 2022 (print) | LCC BJ1475 (ebook) | DDC 177/.7--dc23
LC record available at https://lccn.loc.gov/2021041763
LC ebook record available at https://lccn.loc.gov/2021041764

Typeset in Minion Pro by Hewer Text UK Ltd, Edinburgh
Printed and bound by CPI Group (UK) Ltd, Croydon CR0 4YY

Contents

Introduction: Care and Self-Care

In contemporary societies the most widespread mode of work is care work. The securing of human lives is regarded by our civilization as its supreme goal. Foucault was right when he described modern states as biopolitical. Their main function is to take care of the physical well-being of their populations. In this sense, medicine has taken the place of religion, and the hospital has replaced the Church. The body rather than the soul is the privileged object of institutionalized care: 'health replaced salvation'.[1] Physicians assumed the role of priests because they are supposed to know our bodies better than we do – much as the priests claimed to know our souls better than we did. However, the care of human bodies goes far beyond medicine in the narrow sense of this word. State institutions do not only care for our bodies as such, but also for the housing, food and other factors that are relevant for keeping our bodies healthy – for example, public and private transportation systems take care of the passengers' bodies being delivered to their destinations undamaged, while the ecological industry takes care of the environment to make it more fitted for human health.

Religion cared not only for the life of the soul in this world but also for its fate after it had left its body. The same can be said about contemporary, secularized institutions of care. Our culture is permanently producing extensions of our material bodies: photographs, documents, videos, copies of our letters and emails and other artefacts. And we participate in this process by producing books, artworks, films, websites and Instagram accounts. All these objects and documents are kept for some time after our death. That means that, instead of a spiritual after-life for our souls, our care institutions are securing the material after-life of our bodies. We take care of cemeteries, museums, libraries, historical archives, public monuments and places of

1 Michel Foucault, *The Birth of the Clinic*, London: Routledge, 1973, p.198.

historical significance. We preserve cultural identity, historical memory and traditional urban spaces and ways of life. Every individual is included in this system of extended care. Our extended bodies can be called 'symbolic bodies'. They are symbolic not because they are somehow 'immaterial' but because they allow us to inscribe our physical bodies into the system of care. Similarly, the Church could not care for an individual soul before its body was baptized and named.

Indeed, protection of our living bodies is mediated by our symbolic bodies. Thus, when we go to a physician, we have to present a passport or other identity papers. These papers describe our bodies and their history: male or female, place and date of birth, colour of hair and eyes, biometric photographs. Beyond that we must indicate our postal address, phone number and email address. We must also present our health insurance card or arrange to pay privately. That presupposes that we can prove that we have a bank account, a profession and workplace, or a pension or some other relevant social benefits. Not accidentally, when we go to see a physician, they start by asking us to fill out a huge mass of different documents, including a history of our previous illnesses, and sign our consent to eventual disclosure of our private data and waivers concerning all the consequences of our treatment. The doctor examines all this documentation before examining our bodies. In many cases, physicians do not examine our physical bodies at all – the examination of documentation seems to be sufficient. That demonstrates that the care of our physical bodies and their health is integrated into a much bigger system of surveillance and care that controls our symbolic bodies. And one suspects that this system is less interested in our individual health and survival than in its own smooth functioning. Indeed, the death of an individual does not change a lot in its symbolic body – it leads only to the issuing of the certificate of death and some additional papers related to the funeral procedure, positioning of the grave, design of a coffin or urn and other similar arrangements. There are only slight changes in our symbolic bodies that turn them in symbolic corpses.

It seems that the system of care objectifies us as patients, turns us into living corpses and treats us as sick animals and not as autonomous human beings. However, fortunately or unfortunately, this impression is far from the truth. In fact, the medical system does not objectify but rather subjectifies us. First of all, this system begins to care about an individual body only if the patient appeals to this system because he or she feels unwell, sick, ill. Indeed, the first question that one is asked when one goes to a physician is: What can I do for you? In other words, medicine understands itself as a service and treats the patient as a customer. Patients must decide not only if they are ill or not but also which parts of their bodies are ill, because medicine is highly specialized and it is the patient who has to make the initial choice of the appropriate medical institution and type of doctor. Patients are the primary caretakers of their bodies. The medical system of care is secondary. Self-care precedes care.

We seek salvation through medicine only when we feel ill – but not when we feel well. However, if we do not have any special medical knowledge we have only a vague understanding of how our body works. Indeed, we do not have any 'innate' ability 'internally', through self-contemplation, to establish the difference between being healthy or sick. We can feel unwell but be actually quite healthy, and we can feel OK and yet be terminally ill. The knowledge about our bodies comes from outside. Our illnesses also come from outside – as genetically predetermined or produced through infections, bad food or climate. All the advice about how to improve the functioning of our bodies and make them healthier also comes from outside – be it sport or all possible kinds of alternative therapy or diet. In other words, to take care of our own physical body means, for us, to take care of something we know more or less nothing about.

As with everything in our world, the medical system is not really a system but a field of competition. When one informs oneself about the medical treatment that is good for one's health, one discovers soon enough that the medical authorities oppose each other on all the important issues. The medical advice that one gets is mostly contradictory. At the same time, all this advice looks very professional, and so it is difficult to choose a course of treatment without having any special medical knowledge and professional background. The seriousness of the choice is stressed, though, by the obligation of the patient to give consent to a particular treatment – taking into consideration and accepting all the possible negative consequences of this treatment, including death. This means that, although medicine presents itself as a science, the choice of a particular medical treatment by the patient presupposes an irrational leap of faith. It is irrational because the basis of medical knowledge is the investigation of corpses. One cannot really investigate the inner structure and workings of the living body. The body must die to become really known. Or at least it should be anesthetized. Thus, I cannot know my body because I cannot investigate myself as a corpse. And I cannot simultaneously anesthetize and operate on myself. I even cannot see the internal condition of my body without using X-rays or CT scans. The doctor's medical knowledge is transcendent to my knowledge of myself. And my relation to the transcendent can be only faith – not knowledge.

The proposals concerning the state of one's body come not only from medical schools but also from the various alternative healing practices, including sport, wellness, fitness, yoga and tai chi, as well as different types of diet. All of them require from us a leap of faith. In this respect, it is interesting to watch advertisements for prescription drugs on American TV. These advertisements are mostly truly mysterious. One sees happy couples, often with children, eating together and laughing, playing tennis or golf. From time to time, one sees a strange-looking word that is probably supposed to be the name of the advertised drug. But it is mostly unclear what kind of illnesses is cured by this drug and how that drug should be used. The whole advert looks totally improbable because all the people showed in the video are obviously in good health. It might seem that the only thing that can make them ill is the advertised drug itself. Even if it is not quite clear what this drug is good for, at the end one sees a short list of its side effects. Usually, the list runs from dizziness and vomiting to blindness and occasional death. After a couple of moments, the list disappears and the video shows the happy family again. The viewer is relieved that this family has remained healthy and happy – probably because it has decided not to take this drug after all.

We are accustomed to equate knowledge with power. We think that the subject of knowledge is a strong, powerful subject – a potentially universal, imperial subject. But as a caretaker of my physical and symbolic bodies I am not a subject of knowledge. As I noted earlier, I do not have knowledge of my physical body. But I also do not have full knowledge of my symbolic body. At the origin of my symbolic body – of my identity – is the birth certificate that informs me of my name, the names of my parents, the date and place of my birth, my citizenship and other details. It is the basic document that later generates all other documents, such as my passport, different addresses and educational certificates. All these documents, taken together, define my status and place in the society – they reflect the way in which the society sees and appreciates me. And they define the way in which I will be remembered after my death. At the same time, I did not experience my conception by my parents, the event of my birth, the time and place of my birth and the act of receiving my citizenship. My identity is the work of others.

Of course, I can try to change my symbolic body in different ways – from changing my gender to writing the books that explain that I am, actually, quite different from how I appear to others. However, to change gender, one has to go to surgeons, and to publish books one has to present them to editors and ask for their opinion. Or one has to put these books on the internet and ask for the opinion of users. In other words, one cannot obtain full control over the changes of one's own symbolic body. Additionally, symbolic bodies go through a permanent process of re-evaluation. What was symbolically valuable yesterday can become devalued today and revalued tomorrow. In the role of caretaker, one cannot control or even influence these processes. Beyond that, in our current civilization we are permanently surveilled and recorded without our knowledge and consent. The symbolic body is an archive of documents, images, videos, sound recordings, books and other data. The results of the surveillance are a part of this archive

– even if these results are unknown to the surveilled. This archive is material – and exists even if nobody, including the surveilled, has access to it or is interested in it. In this respect, it is very informative to watch what happens when somebody commits a crime – especially a politically motivated crime. Suddenly, one finds the images of the suspected criminals as they buy food in a food store or take money from an ATM – together with written manifestoes or a collection of arms. This example shows that the emergence and growth of a symbolic body is a process that is relatively independent of social attention and takes place mostly beyond the control of the primary caretaker of this symbolic body. After the death of the primary caretaker, the machine of caring does not stop. And this machine demonstrates that the efforts of the primary caretaker to shape the symbolic body has had only limited success. The inscription on the grave mostly reproduces the birth certificate plus the date of death and only cursory information about the ways in which the caretakers tried to become what they were not – like writer, painter, revolutionary. The re-evaluations of symbolic bodies continue after the death of their caretakers – the monuments are erected, destroyed and re-erected, the books are published, burnt and then republished, new documents emerge, other documents are lost. The care continues – but, in a strange way, the responsibility for posthumous changes in the re-evaluations of the individual's symbolic body remains attributed to its primary caretaker. And, indeed, the care for the symbolic body presupposes the anticipation of its fate after the death of the physical body – as the care for the physical body presupposes the expectation of its unavoidable death.

It is this combination of the physical and symbolic bodies that we call our Self. As a caretaker of the Self, the subject takes an external position towards it. The subject is not central, but is also not decentred. It is, as Helmuth Plessner rightly says, 'eccentric'.[2] I know that I am the subject of self-care because I have learnt it from others – just

2 Helmuth Plessner, *Levels of Organic Life and the Human*, New York: Fordham University Press, 2019, pp. 267ff.

as I learnt my name, my nationality and other personal details. However, to be a subject of self-care does not mean to have a right to decide about the practice of care. As a patient, I am required to follow all the instructions of the doctors and endure passively all the painful procedures to which I am subjected. In this case, to practise self-care means to turn oneself into an object of care. And this work of self-objectification requires a strong will, discipline and determination. If I fail to fulfil all my obligations as a patient, this is interpreted as a lack of will, as weakness.

On the other hand, the decision by a healthy person to ignore all reasonable advice and to take the risk of death is admired by our society. The sick are supposed to choose life, but the healthy are welcomed to choose death. That is obvious in the case of war. But we also admire intense work effort that might damage the health of the worker. And we admire the practitioners of extreme sports and adventures that can lead to their death. In other words, what is favourable for the symbolic body can ruin the physical body. To enhance the social status of our symbolic bodies often means an investment of our life energy that potentially ruins our health and even involves a risk of death.

Thus, the eccentric subject of self-care has to take care of the distribution of care between physical and symbolic bodies. For example, the health criteria appropriate for a professional athlete cannot be applied to somebody who is not involved in professional sport. The same can be said about other professions that are dependent on physical or manual work. But the so-called intellectual professions are also dependent on the health of their practitioners – not everybody is able to sit many hours in an office, not everybody can stay focused on a certain problem for a long period of time. In this sense, we never know what is truly good for our health – to choose a treatment that fits our needs dictated by our symbolic status or to change this status, to choose a different profession, different country, different identity, different family, or no family at all. All these choices are interrelated – and all of them can be helpful or damaging to our health.

Of course, the solution to this problem is often seen in the search for the 'true Self' that is supposed to be situated beyond our physical and symbolic bodies. However, here again one is confronted with different and often contradictory advice and methods – from Cartesian doubt to transcendental meditation. The subject of self-care is constituted through the mode in which we are addressed by society, including the institutions of care. The subject cares for its physical and symbolic bodies because it is required to do so. The requirement to be healthy is the basic and universal requirement directed towards the contemporary subject. Of course, human bodies have different characteristics depending on sex, ethnic origin and other factors. But the requirement to remain healthy applies to all these bodies to the same degree. Only if a body remains healthy can its subject contribute to the well-being of society – or to changing the society. The investment in health is the basic investment that one makes to be able to participate in social life. That is why society tends to reject all forms of decadence, passivity, cultivation of one's own illnesses and unwillingness to practise the usual work of self-care.

In fact, the work of care, including self-care, is always hard work and one is always happy to avoid it. Basically, it is Sisyphean work. Everybody knows that. Every day, food is prepared and then eaten, and then one has to begin to prepare food again. Every day, the room is cleaned – and the next day it should be cleaned again. Every morning and evening, one should brush one's teeth – and the next day, repeat the same ritual. Every day, the state has to protect itself from its enemies – and the next day the situation is the same. A pilot successfully delivers passengers to their destination – and then has to fly back. And, yes, every patient who is treated by the medical system inevitably dies at some point, and so the system begins with the next patient and then comes to the same result. The work of care and self-care is unproductive, remains forever unfinished, and, thus, can be only deeply frustrating. However, it is the most basic and necessary work. Everything else depends on it. Our social, economic and political system treats the population as a source of renewable energy, like the energy of the sun or of wind. However, the generation of this energy is guaranteed not 'naturally' but through the readiness of every individual in the population to practise self-care and to invest in their health. If the population began to neglect this requirement, the whole system would collapse. The eccentric subject of self-care takes a metaposition in its relationship to the social system and in doing so discovers its power. By disinvesting its energy and health, the individual lowers the energy level of the society as a whole. And this metaposition is a universal position: the eccentricity of an individual subject of self-care makes it universal because all the subjects of care of all the Selves find themselves in the same position.

Medical care is often seen as having as its goal the repair of our bodies – to make them able to work and thereby ensure the smooth functioning of society. But our contemporary system of care also treats the bodies that will never be economically functional again and were perhaps not ever functional. In this case the subject is no longer the private owner of its body, who is free to use this body as property and tool. The body becomes fully socialized, bureaucratized and politicized. All its most private, intimate functions, including its reproductive functions, become matters of public interest and political discussion. This is the end of privacy as it has been understood for a long time. But also the subject of self-care is only a participant in the process of political and administrative decisions concerning its own body. The public, symbolic, mediatized body begins to coincide with the physical, private, intimate body. One can see this equation of public and intimate in contemporary social media and, in general, on the internet. The internet functions as a medium of satisfaction of our most everyday and intimate needs and desires and, at the same time, as the medium of their inscription in digital memory – making them potentially publicly accessible. This loss of privacy provokes calls for its restoration. However, a return to privacy – that is, a return to the unrestricted private ownership of the body – would be ruinous for the system of care.

The active participation of the subject of self-care in the medical, political and administrative discussions concerning its body presupposes its ability to judge the knowledge about that care, including the medical knowledge, from a position of non-knowledge. Different scientific schools are competing for recognition, influence, fame and power. All of them claim to care about an individual from the position of knowledge. The individual subject has to make a choice among them without having the knowledge necessary to make this choice. That makes it feel weak and disoriented. But this weakness is, at the same time, a strength, because every kind of knowledge becomes powerful only if it is accepted and practised. The philosophical tradition can be understood as the tradition of reflection on this ambivalence of weakness and strength. The different philosophical teachings suggest the different types of relationship between care and self-care – between dependence and autonomy. Let us undertake a short survey of these teachings to better understand the genealogy of the contemporary state of this relationship.

1

From Care to Self-Care

The paradoxical situation of judging knowledge from the position of non-knowledge is first described in Plato's dialogues. Socrates was an attentive and interested listener of the Sophistic discourses offering him different answers to the questions: What is truth? and What is the correct way of life? Thus, Socrates finds himself in a metaposition of choice among these discourses. Now, one would expect Socrates to try to overcome his initial state of non-knowledge – to learn, to become knowledgeable. That is what is usually expected from somebody who does not know – that he or she learns. However, Socrates disappoints these expectations: instead of going forward on the way to the accumulation of knowledge, he takes a step back and rejects the knowledge that he already has. Socrates does not only distrust any teachings that the Sophists propagate but also the Greek tradition of mythology, poetry and tragedy that predisposes the listeners to find the Sophistic discourses persuasive. In other words, Socrates distances himself from and takes an eccentric position towards Greek cultural identity in its totality. The movement of philosophy is not a movement forward, not a progress on the road to education and knowledge, but a movement back, a regression towards a state of non-knowledge. Socrates does not learn and does not teach. He does not want to acquire knowledge, nor does he want to propagate it.

Socrates famously compared himself to a midwife who helps another woman deliver a child. In the same way, Socrates claimed to help the truth to be born in the soul of another person if this person was pregnant with truth. It is obviously a medical metaphor – the care of truth is here understood in analogy to the care for the human body. Being pregnant with truth and giving birth to it is a painful experience: 'Dire are the pangs which my art is able to arouse and to allay in those who consort with me, just like the pangs of women in childbirth; night and day they are full of perplexity and travail which is even worse than that of the women.'[1] When the truth is born, Socrates' patient feels himself relieved. However, this truth can be rejected by Socrates as being false: 'And if I abstract and expose your first-born, because I discover upon inspection that the conception which you have formed is a vain shadow, do not quarrel with me on that account, as the manner of women is when their first children are taken from them. For I have actually known some who were ready to bite me when I deprived them of a darling folly'.[2]

Here the desire for truth is placed on a quasi-physiological level. The patients suffer because they desire the truth. So they go to the Sophists, to the teachers, because they expect to receive the truth from them. Socrates, though, believes that that is the wrong diagnosis: actually, the patients are already pregnant with the truth but cannot deliver it. The truth is not beyond but rather within us – a line of reasoning that became very familiar. The question, however, is this: Does the original internal pressure to receive or deliver the truth emerge in individuals independently of the society in which they live? The whole context of Plato's dialogues suggests that that is not the case. The desire for the truth is imposed on individuals by the society in which they live. The individual is attacked from all sides by different Sophistic discourses and is under the obligation to position itself in the field of knowledge – as a follower of this or that famous teacher. The Socratic method is seductive because it allows the patients to avoid this positioning by claiming that they already have their truth within them – even if this truth remains hidden.

Indeed, even today if one rejects certain philosophical teachings and social projects one is usually asked: And what are your own convictions and projects? Socrates taught us how to avoid this rhetorical trap. One should not say: I reject your opinions. One should just

---

1 Plato, *Theaetetus*, trans. Benjamin Jowett, 1871, Global Grey ebooks, 2018, p. 13.
2 Ibid.

ask: Could you explain your opinions and arguments in more detail? And maybe you can see that there are some contradictions in your argument? This defensive strategy causes every persuasive speech to collapse internally and, at the same time, avoids the requirement to formulate a counter-argument. Of course, this kind of defence is irritating because society wants its members to formulate explicitly their positions related at least to the main problems of public life. To say, 'I have no position at all' looks like an insult. And Socrates, as we know, was sentenced to death because of this insult. The decision of the court was not without certain logic: a man who has no political and ethical positions is already socially dead. What is overlooked here is this: that Socrates – at least in Plato's interpretation – believed that, in the ideal society, nobody will be in need of any individual position. An individual position is always an expression of personal interests. These are primarily economic interests and/or loyalty to one's family. But, in an ideal state, as described in Plato's *Politeia* (*The Republic*), nobody has private property and familial loyalties. It is a state at zero-level. Such a state is eternal because, historically, the relationships of property change and familial structures also change – but their absence cannot change.

This state should be ruled by philosophers who see the true, the good, the right and the beautiful as such and are able to compare these true images to the reality that surrounds them. Philosophy does not take here the form of a teaching, of a discourse. The contemplation of the eternal Good happens in silence. In his famous parable of the cave from *Politeia*, Plato's Socrates insists that one must to be put under external pressure to be brought to the contemplation of truth. The social space is compared to a cave. Originally, one is sitting with one's face to the wall, seeing the shadows of the things that are carried in different directions at the entrance of the cave. The impulse to discover the origin of these shadows has to come from outside, one has to be forced to change the position of one's body: 'At first, when any of them is liberated and compelled suddenly to stand up and turn his neck round and walk and look towards the light, he will suffer sharp pains; the glare will distress him, and he will be unable to see the realities of which in his former state he had seen the shadows.'[3] The event of evidence does not happen momentarily but as a result of the further application of violence: 'And suppose once more, that he is reluctantly dragged up a steep and rugged ascent, and held fast until he's forced into the presence of the sun himself, is he not likely to be pained and irritated? When he approaches the light his eyes will be dazzled, and he will not be able to see anything at all of what are now called realities.'[4] Here, it is important to see that this violence is applied to the whole body of the patient/student because they cannot turn their eyes to the truth without turning their whole body. The whole scene of the conversion to the philosophical mode of existence is a terrifying story – true horror.

Indeed, the individual soul is brought to the vision of the eternal light not through persuasion or its own arbitrary decision but as an effect of the changed position of its body produced by the direct application of physical violence. To speak in Marxist terms, the subject sees the light not as a result of spiritual awakening on the level of the superstructure but due to the shift of the position of its body on the level of the material base. Not surprisingly, Badiou stresses the violence of this act of materialistic metanoia in his 'translation' of Plato's *Republic*:

> His eyes hurt horribly, he wants to run away, he wants to go back to what he can endure seeing, those shadows whose being he considers a lot more real than that of the objects they're showing him. But all of a sudden a bunch of tough guys in our pay grab him and drag him roughly through the aisles of the movie theater. They make him go through a little side door that was hidden up till then. They throw him into a filthy tunnel through which you emerge into the open air, onto a sunlit mountainside in spring. Dazzled by the light, he covers his eyes with a trembling hand; our agents push him up the steep slope, for a long time, higher and higher! Still higher! They finally get

---

3 Plato, *The Republic*, trans. Benjamin Jowett, New York: Vintage, 1991, p. 254.
4 Ibid., p. 254.

to the top, in full sun, and there they release him, run back down the mountain and disappear.[5]

But does this painful exercise make the philosopher a better member of society? Not at all. When the philosopher – blinded by the light of truth – comes back into the cave, 'men would say of him that up he went and down he came without his eyes; and that it was better not even to think ascending and if any one tried to loose another and lead him up to the light, let them only catch the offender, and they would put him to death.'[6]

However, the perspective of death does not frighten the philosopher. In the eternal light of truth, he discovers that his soul is eternal. The contemplation of the eternal idea of the Good guarantees to philosophers their eccentric position towards their own bodies and the social body as a whole. Thus, they can turn themselves from objects of care into the subjects of care and self-care. Plato does not say explicitly who drags one of the cave dwellers out of the cave – just as he does not identify the workers moving the objects back and forth at the entrance to the cave. In any case, it becomes clear that the subject itself is too weak to develop an initiative in matters of truth. It can achieve truth – but only under external guidance and control. But why is it so weak? Plato would say: because it is imprisoned inside its body. This imprisonment makes the soul too preoccupied by corporeal desires and everyday interests. And that makes the soul weak. The philosophical care of truth presupposes removal of bodily desires, pragmatic calculations and personal obligations. The truth shows itself when everything that is related to the body and its social status is removed and the soul becomes able to contemplate itself. That is why philosophy is the preparation for death – for leaving the cave of earthly, corporeal existence. And the preparation for death is a lonely and quiet activity – it is the activity of contemplation.

5 Alain Badiou, *Plato's Republic: A Dialogue in Sixteen Chapters*, trans. Susan Spitzer, Cambridge: Polity Press, 2012, p. 24.

6 Ibid., p. 255.

The Platonic philosopher avoids struggle and competition. The Sophists compete for fame and money, but the philosopher is already tired of this competition and only watches it. The philosopher is ready to make a couple of ironic remarks about this spectacle of competition – and that is all. The light of truth cannot be articulated and presented in the form of teaching. However, Socrates did not remain silent. He did not try to escape from public space and public view. He did not go to live in the woods or the desert. Instead, he remained very much a part of the social life of Athens. He continued participating in public gatherings and Sophistic disputes. But having reached point zero of opinions, Socrates was confronted with the task of developing a zero discourse – a discourse without content. What was the goal of this zero discourse if it did not have as its goal to inform, influence and persuade? Its goal was not to persuade but to dissuade – for Plato's Socrates the evidence of truth is an effect of the elimination of all the false opinions. The same can be said about the experience of evidence to which Descartes appeals in asserting the truth of his famous *cogito ergo sum*.

The experience of evidence is, obviously, merely 'subjective' experience. That is why the evidence needs a confirmation of its truth status by the same caretaker who put the individual in the position of access to truth – by the midwife, to use the Socrates' comparison. Historically, it was the Church that took on this role of universal caretaker. The Church reorganized the everyday life of the European population down to the smallest details with the goal of turning it towards the contemplation of God – and it examined the results of individual contemplations to establish whether the corresponding evidence was true or false. Later, in post-Cartesian times, the Church was replaced by the scientific community that had the same role to control the personal evidences. In other words, here self-care is understood as an effect of institutional care, the eccentricity of self-care remains subjected to the institutions of care.

To become truly eccentric, the subject of self-care has to insist on the validity of his or her personal evidence – even against the judgement of the Church or the scientific community. For Plato, the light of truth could be obscured by the imprisonment of the soul in the body but not simulated or falsified. However, in the Christian tradition the light that seems to be truth can be demonic – Lucifer is one of the names of Satan. One has to choose – not between light and darkness but between two lights. And the decision to choose the wrong light can be easily understood as the triumph of the freedom of the subject of self-care – even if such a choice is risky and can lead to eternal perdition. During the Romantic period, many intellectuals and poets were ready to identify themselves with Mephistopheles, the Devil and Satan, that is, with all forms of negation and rebellion – only to get free from the protective oppression of institutionalized Christianity. One turned from God to freedom. But what about health? Is the search for freedom good or bad for our health?

2

From Self-Care to Care

One can argue that this question is at the centre of Hegel's philosophy. History is understood here as a process of revealing freedom as the essence of human subjectivity. The movement of history follows its own inner logic – the logic of the revelation of freedom. The philosopher is not a teacher, caretaker or leader but a spectator of this movement. Not unlike Plato's Socrates, the philosopher can identify when the search for freedom has come to an end, when it has become successful. Throughout history, freedom manifests itself as negation. Freedom is demonic, if you will. Subjectivity will know its truth when it goes through the whole history of negations of everything that was historically established and institutionalized. At the end of the violent history of revolutions and wars, the human spirit will establish its own law. Then subjectivity will live in its own world – and not in the world imposed on it by the powers of the past.

Not accidentally, Hegel speaks about human history as the Golgotha of the spirit. The truth of subjectivity should demonstrate itself 'phenomenologically', which means becoming visible by manifesting itself in historical action – as divine subjectivity manifested itself through the death of Christ on the cross. Human history is the history of the liberation of subjectivity from the obscurity and burden of things as they are. The goal of this liberation is to demonstrate subjectivity as it is, as freedom. History is thus a teleological and guided process – guided by the dialectical logic of negation of negation. But, contrary to role of the Christian Church, we have here to do with guidance without protection. History guides us to the truth, but if it protected us we would never get access to this truth – our subjectivity would never be fully manifested. Hegel celebrates opposition, protest and revolt. However, for him they are justified only if they are successful – and they are successful only if they correspond to the progressive movement of history and take place at the right historical moment. But who is to decide which particular historical action is opportune and which is not? It is a decision not of the historical agent but of history itself. And this decision becomes evident only after the action has been taken, not before. As a phenomenologist, Hegel takes up the position of spectator of the historical movement. He is not a spectator of souls but a spectator of bodies in action – of the body of God suffering on the cross but also of the bodies mobilized by the historical progress in their fight for their freedom.

Hegel saw the ultimate self-revelation of subjectivity in the terror of the French Revolution. The universality of this terror demonstrated that the truth of subjectivity is freedom. Thus, the French Revolution became the ultimate historical revelation of human subjectivity and, at the same time, the end of history: 'In this absolute freedom all social groups and classes which are the spiritual spheres into which the whole is articulated are abolished; the individual consciousness that belonged to any such sphere, and willed and fulfilled itself in it, has put aside its limitation; its purpose is the general purpose, its language universal law, its work is universal work.'[1] And, further:

> Universal Freedom, therefore, can produce neither a positive work, nor a deed; there is left for it only a negative action; it is merely a *fury* of destruction ... The sole work and deed of universal freedom is therefore *death*, a death too which has no inner significance or filling, for what is negated is the empty point of the absolutely free self. It is just the coldest and meanest of all deaths, which no more significance than cutting off a head of cabbage or swallowing a mouthful of water.[2]

This death does not translate the individuals into the Heaven of Christianity – but also has no utility in the sense of Enlightenment, bringing no riches and no fame.

1 G. W. F. Hegel, *Phenomenology of the Spirit*, trans. A. V. Miller, Oxford: Oxford University Press, 1977, p. 357.

2 Ibid., pp. 359–60.

This is why, after the revelation of their universal freedom as universal terror, the individuals return to their particular roles, to their particular conditions and limited tasks – in other words, they return to culture. However, it is not a simple return to the pre-revolutionary culture that would rejuvenate the established order – and then leave a possibility of the revolutionary explosion being repeated again. Revolutionary terror teaches the individuals fear of death as 'their absolute master'.[3] The post-revolutionary fear of death is, therefore, not the same as the pre-revolutionary fear of God. The individual now knows death not as an external danger but as the work of its own freedom. In this sense, the negativity of freedom becomes positive: now the individual knows itself – as this knowledge becomes its essence.[4]

The end of history is reached. Historical action has become senseless. After the French Revolution, every individual knows about itself everything it has to know. Namely, it knows that it has to fear itself. History was the history of negation – and ended with the negation of negation, with the return of the individual to its particular place and its re-inscription into a system of government and administration. This system of government can present itself as an embodiment of freedom but that is a false claim:

> Neither by the mere idea of obedience to *self-given* laws which would assign to it only a part of the whole, nor by its being *represented* in law-making and universal action, does self-consciousness let itself be cheated out of reality, the reality of *itself* making the law and accomplishing, not a particular work, but the universal work itself. For where the self is merely *represented* and is present only as an idea, there it is not *actual*; where it is represented by proxy, it *is not*. . .[5]

The historical moment of the revelation of freedom remains behind us.

3 Ibid., p. 361.
4 Ibid., p. 363.
5 Ibid., p. 359.

The historical human was dangerous – mobilized by history and remembered in historical chronicles. Human history was a history of negation moved by the desire for freedom. At the same time, it was a history of reason that negated the powers, authorities and beliefs that were irrational because their only legitimation was tradition, the power of the past. But, after the end of history, the paths of freedom and reason parted. Post-revolutionary social and political institutions became reasonable institutions – and so the radical negation of them could be only irrational, destructive. Reason coincides now with the strategy of self-preservation. As a reasonable being, the post-revolutionary, post-historical being has been doomed to become a demobilized, domesticated being. Thus, it becomes clear why the Hegelian 'end of history' made the next generations so nervous. After the end of history, humans lost the chance to become heroic and worthy of historical memory. Reason acted no longer as negation of the existing order but as the legitimization of the status quo. Now to be a reasonable man meant avoiding mortal risk, preventing violent death, and thus wars and revolutions. There were no more historic goals for which one should be ready to sacrifice one's life. Instead, the only activity that one could practise remained self-preservation. The philosopher who earlier acted as a quasi-divine spectator of history became a guardian of the post-historical state. Once again, the philosopher operated by anamnesis but it was not the anamnesis of the eternal truth but rather historical anamnesis that told the history of historical illusions and failures. The goal of this historical anamnesis was to dissuade the listener or reader from repeating the errors of the past – errors that could at one point in history have been truths but became irrelevant after the end of history. One had to remember history only to avoid its repetition.

Of course, one can always argue that the history of liberation did not come to an end, that we still are confronted with violence, war, oppression and revolution. However, that is not the point here. The real question is whether, if the end of history as revelation of human freedom was achieved, the only goal of civilization would remain the preservation of individual human bodies secured by the rule of law?

The highly mobilized, historical bodies of war and revolution would then become the demobilized bodies of care. The spirit would abandon them – they would no longer be ready to put their lives in peril in the name of ideas, projects and utopias directed to the future because all these ideas and utopias remained in the past. The role of the Church was now overtaken by the post-historical state that had become a 'pastoral' state, to use Foucault's term. The goal of this state is not a contemplation of truth but the health of the population. The absolute master of the modern, secular, post-revolutionary state is indeed death. The state protects the bodies of its citizens from self-inflicted death – from the destructive freedom that is the essence of their subjectivities. In this way, the state prevents the individuals from taking control of death, from becoming the masters of death – through crime, war or revolution. The post-historical society is the society of total protection, total care. But this care, which protects humans from themselves, delivers them to natural death. In this sense, death remains the absolute master of the post-historical state.

However, there is something overlooked here: the human body is not merely a socialized body of care. And it is not only natural death that humans share with animals and plants. Humans share with them generational change, the participation in the universal chain of deaths and births. And humans go through the same cycle of being young, energetic and full of desires, projects and plans towards becoming old, weak, disappointed, demotivated – and then dying. So it seems that mobilization and demobilization of our bodies happen at the lowest, bodily level of our existence. Those are not so much the effects of our participation in the history of political struggles as the manifestations of the vital cycle of our lives. Here history is recognized as secondary to generational change.

This means that the system of care and protection of our bodies isolates these bodies from the universal flows of vital energies. In fact, these energies are suppressed by the system of care. It is the paradox of the biopolitical state: it has the goal to make us healthy but, actually, makes us sick. Indeed, only the sick persons need care. By taking care of its whole population the biopolitical state treats everybody as sick and distributes care according to the system of hierarchies and ranks that defines the place of individual symbolic bodies. The symbolic body is the documented, historically objectified and bureaucratically situated soul. Plato's soul was imprisoned inside the body. The post-Hegelian bodies are imprisoned inside their souls that became their symbolic bodies. So now it is not our spiritual freedom but, rather, our health, our pure vital energy that pushes us against the boundaries of our symbolic bodies and negates the modern, pastoral, biopolitical state and its mechanisms of protection.

3

Great Health

As is well known, Nietzsche undertook the 're-evaluation of all values' – an intellectual operation that basically consisted in replacing the search for the truth with the desire to become healthy. This substitution was an act of radical democratization of philosophy. Indeed, not everybody is interested in theoretical discussions and the search for truth, but almost everybody wants to be healthy rather than sick. The central question here, of course, is what it means to be healthy. For Nietzsche, to be healthy did not merely mean that a body has been recognized as healthy through a medical examination. According to Nietzsche, the manifestation of health is aggression. Here one can see an analogy to the Hegelian notion of freedom, which manifests itself as negation of an existing order. But there is also an important difference – and it is precisely this difference that radically separates Nietzsche's philosophy of health from Hegel's philosophy of freedom. The healthy organism is aggressive because health means energy – and energy manifests itself in action that creates for this organism a place in the world. Thus, health is aggressive because it affirms itself and strives to dominate its environment. Health is not negative, its actions are not motivated by *ressentiment* and protest. Therefore, freedom is dialectical but health is not. Freedom becomes self-affirmative at the end of history when it negates itself. But health is self-affirmative from the beginning.

Indeed, as we saw, the essence of pure freedom is nothingness; its manifestation is simple destruction. The return to order means the self-denial of freedom – the negation of negation. That is why Nietzsche saw the struggle for freedom as a manifestation of nihilism and decadence. Aggressive health, on the contrary, fights not for nothing, or for no-order, but to impose a new order. The subject of this fight can lose the battle but it will never be ready to accept a new slavery – as post-historical European humanity is. This conception of health could appear a bit too romantic, but it is not easy to avoid – even in the narrow context of medical studies. Thus, Georges Canguilhem, after discussing different definitions of health, writes:

> If we now move back from these analyses to the concrete feeling of the state they are trying to define, we will understand that for man health is a feeling of assurance in life to which no limit is fixed. *Valere*, from which value derives, means to be in good health in Latin. Health is a way of tackling existence as one feels that one is not only possessor or bearer but also, if necessary, creator of value, establisher of vital norms.[1]

On the other hand, weakening of the will to power can make one sick. Thus, Canguilhem writes further:

> In the long run a malaise arises from not being sick in a world where there are sick men. And what if this were not because one is stronger than the disease or stronger than others, but simply because the occasion has not presented itself? And what if, in the end, when the occasion does arise, one were to show oneself as weak, as unprepared as, or perhaps more so than others? Thus there arises in the normal man an anxiety about having remained normal, a need for disease as a test of health, that is, as its proof, an unconscious search for disease, a provocation of it. Normal man's disease is the appearance of a fault in his biological confidence in himself.[2]

Here, 'normal' obviously means healthy.

In his *Ecce Homo*, Nietzsche professes absolute biological confidence in himself. In this sense, it is his most authentically modern book. According to Nietzsche, one has to have 'healthy instincts'. Then one is able to act in a way that makes one's body healthier – and reject

---

1 Georges Canguilhem, *The Normal and the Pathological*, New York: Zone Books, 1991, p. 201.

2 Ibid., p. 286.

everything that makes it sick. Thus, Nietzsche insists on the necessity of making the right choice concerning nutrition and climate. A long and beautiful quotation:

> To the question of nutrition, that of locality and climate is next of kin. Nobody is so constituted as to be able to live everywhere and anywhere; and he who has great duties to perform, which lay claim to all his strength, has, in this respect, a very limited choice. The influence of climate upon the bodily functions, affecting their acceleration or retardation, extends so far, that a blunder in the choice of locality and climate is able not only to alienate a man from his actual duty, but also to withhold it from him altogether, so that he never even comes face to face with it. Animal vigour never acquires enough strength in him in order to reach that pitch of artistic freedom which makes his own soul whisper to him: I, alone, can do that . . . Ever so slight a tendency to laziness in the intestines, once it has become a habit, is quite sufficient to make something mediocre, something "German" out of a genius; the climate of Germany, alone, is enough to discourage the strongest and most heroically disposed intestines. The tempo of the body's functions is closely bound up with the agility or the clumsiness of the spirit's feet; spirit itself is indeed only a form of these organic functions. Let anybody make a list of the places in which men of great intellect have been found, and are still found; where wit, subtlety, and malice constitute happiness; where genius is almost necessarily at home: all of them rejoice in exceptionally dry air. Paris, Provence, Florence, Jerusalem, Athens – these names prove something, namely: that genius is conditioned by dry air, by a pure sky – that is to say, by rapid organic functions, by the constant and ever-present possibility of procuring for one's self great and even enormous quantities of strength.[3]

So to be healthy means to be strong and full of energy – and this energy should manifest itself in conflict, in war:

---

3 Friedrich Nietzsche, *Ecce Homo*, in *Complete Works*, vol. 17, ed. Oscar Levy, trans. Anthony M. Ludovici, New York: Macmillan, 1911, pp. 33–4.

> At heart I am a warrior. Attacking belongs to my instincts. To be able to be an enemy, to be an enemy – maybe these things presuppose a strong nature; in any case all strong natures involve these things. Such natures need resistance, consequently they go in search of obstacles: the pathos of aggression belongs of necessity to strength as much as the feelings of revenge and of rancour belong to weakness.[4]

Time and again, Nietzsche draws this distinction between attacking from a position of weakness and *ressentiment* and attacking as manifestation of a surplus of energy and health. So, he writes:

> I attack only those things from which all personal differences are excluded, in which any such thing as a background of disagreeable experiences is lacking . On the contrary, attacking is to me a proof of goodwill and, in certain circumstances, of gratitude. By means of it, I do honour to a thing, I distinguish a thing ; whether I associate my name with that of an institution or a person, by being against or for either, is all the same to me. If I wage war against Christianity, I feel justified in doing so, because in that quarter I have met with no fatal experiences and difficulties – the most earnest Christians have always been kindly disposed to me. I, personally, the most essential opponent of Christianity, am far from holding the individual responsible for what is the fatality of long ages.[5]

Nietzsche argues against Christianity because, for him, Christ is a perfect example of decadence – a man of weak will, too sensitive, too nervous, incapable of either defending himself or attacking others. On the contrary, Nietzsche says about himself that he is not a man but dynamite: true health is explosive, dangerous – it destroys the culture that wants to control it. However, even though Nietzsche attacks the dominant order he does not want to change it – such a desire would make his attack merely a means to achieve a certain generalized, abstract goal and thus a

4 Ibid., p. 23.
5 Ibid., p. 24.

decadent act of *ressentiment*. An authentic attack is a manifestation of the health and energy of the attacker here and now. Such an attack has its cause in the will to power – but the will to power understood as a will to become an object of admiration and not the head of an administration. Nietzsche is not interested in 'real power' but in the fame that, as he hopes, his attacks against Christianity and post-Christian humanism will bring him in the future. Indeed, he expects admiration and fame from future humanity much more than from his contemporaries.

Nietzsche thus proclaims that he belongs not to the present but to the future:

> My time has not yet come either; some are born posthumously. One day institutions will be needed in which men will live and teach, as I understand living and teaching; maybe, also, that by that time, chairs will be founded and endowed for the interpretation of Zarathustra. But I should regard it as a complete contradiction of myself, if I expected to find ears and eyes for my truths to-day: the fact that no one listens to me, that no one knows how to receive at my hands to-day, is not only comprehensible, it seems to me quite the proper thing.[6]

Speaking about Zarathustra, Nietzsche says that Zarathustra has 'great health'. To explain the meaning of 'great health' Nietzsche quotes from his own *Gaya Scienza*: We new, nameless, and unfathomable creatures, we firstlings of a future still unproved – we who have a new end in view also require new means to that end, that is to say, a new healthiness, a stronger, keener, tougher, bolder, and merrier healthiness than any that has existed heretofore.[7] 'Nameless' is here the key word – one can see it when Nietzsche discusses great health in connection with poetic inspiration:

> If one had the smallest vestige of superstition left in one, it would hardly be possible completely to set aside the idea that one is the

6 Ibid., p. 55.
7 Ibid., p. 99.

mere incarnation, mouthpiece, or medium of an almighty power. The idea of revelation, in the sense that something which profoundly convulses and upsets one becomes suddenly visible and audible with indescribable certainty and accuracy – describes the simple fact.[8]

These promises of the new, nameless and unheard of, belonging to the future, sound somewhat vague. But they mark the birth of the ideology of creativity that still dominates the individual and social imagination of our time. We all engage in the tedious, monotone, repetitive rituals of everyday life – until death stops us. We all do the work of care that keeps the social institutions functioning. Philosophy and culture in general were always attempts to find a way out of this routine of practical life. Traditionally, the *vita contemplativa* served as the alternative to the *vita activa*: one decided not to work but to contemplate. Now Nietzsche argues that only weak, decadent natures take this decision. Strong natures – those endowed with *great health* – choose the great adventure. They trust their health instincts and replace care with self-care. Today we would say: they become creative. That means: they invent new life-forms, break with traditions and conventions, discover new possibilities of existence, new technology, new art, a new mentality. They have more and not less energy and health than the ordinary population that is immersed in everyday practical life and spends all its energy on keeping things as they are – the population that is sick of caring and being cared for. Creativity is a symptom of great health – but it is also acceptance of death. Creativity is, among other things, risk taking, including mortal risk. One can even say: creativity is nothing else than taking mortal risks. The will to design the future presupposes also the will to design one's own death. Marinetti describes it well in his Futurist manifesto: 'Nothing at all worth dying for, other than the desire to divest ourselves finally of the courage that weighed us down!'[9]

---

8 Ibid., pp. 101–02.

9 Filippo Tommaso Marinetti, *The Manifesto of Futurism*, in *Critical Writings*, ed. Günter Berghaus, trans. Doug Thompson, New York: Farrar, Straus and Giroux, 2006, pp. 11–17.

Explosive Dionysian forces make a dangerous bomb out of the individual body. Death can be understood as the most radical manifestation of exhaustion, lack of energy and weakness. But it can also be a manifestation of energetic overflow, a surplus of anonymous forces that destroy the body as something too particular and limited. The body becomes dissolved in the universal, infinite flow of cosmic energy. But how to distinguish between death from exhaustion and death from surplus of energy? Basically, death from exhaustion is natural death and Dionysian death is violent death. The *élan vital* creates an inner pressure that pushes an individual towards death – instead of patiently waiting for it. One will sacrifice one's life for nothing, because, at the moment of sacrifice, at the moment of taking the risk of death one feels oneself truly alive. Life is understood here as an inner experience. The feeling of being truly alive confronts the subject with evidence that cannot be relativized by any medical knowledge and historical critique. Its intensity is comparable to the intensity of the evidence with which Descartes recognized his doubt as the proof of his existence. For Descartes, the act of negation of all accepted opinions as well as philosophical and scientific teachings was sufficient to certify his existence and at the same time to reveal the universal aspect of this existence. For Nietzsche and Marinetti, this kind of negation was already familiar – a part of the game. True negation had also to be self-negation – negation of the individual that manifests universal life, the infinite cosmic energies and flows. Here again the acceptance of death signals a belief in participation in a reality that transcends death, that is eternal. Only this time this reality is not spirit but life. Spirit operates by negations – and the number of negations is limited. On the contrary, life operates through affirmations and repetitions. Life repeats itself – it is the eternal repetition of the same. Immortality is thought here not as a continuous presence but as a series of repetitions: a very modern form of immortality.

However, the ideology of creativity remains historicist. That does not mean that history is still understood as the history of progress. There is no common, pre-established goal towards which history moves – no ultimate contemplation of truth to which everybody will get access at the end of days. The future is an effect of creative experimentation – of an investment of the extra-health that creative individuals have spent to shape it. In this sense, the future becomes personalized – as indeed are the present and the past. We are living in buildings that were constructed by somebody, using machines that were invented and built by somebody, looking at works of art that were created by somebody. All these creatives used nameless energies but they themselves had names. And we cannot articulate our own position in the world without evoking and using these names. The ideology of creativity excludes the possibility of referring to God's will or to the historical movement of the Absolute Spirit. Nietzsche saw history as 'monumental history' – as a chain of the 'great men' who fought their 'great struggles'. These struggles may have been the struggles of the past:

> But one thing will live, the monogram of their most essential being, a work, an act, a piece of rare enlightenment, a creation. It will live because posterity cannot do without it. In this transfigured form, fame is something more that the tastiest morsel of our *amour propre*, as Schopenhauer called it. It is the belief in the solidarity and continuity of the greatness of all ages and a protest against the passing away of generations and the transitoriness of things.[10]

Earlier, it was God who guaranteed the unity and continuity of times. Now it is the transhistorical fame of the creative few.

Although Hegel's *Phenomenology* describes history as the history of negations and destructions, the *Phenomenology* itself remains dependent on the stability of historical archives – on their preservation and good administration. In other words, Hegelian dialectics relies on the work of care that transcends it. It is, of course, not the medical care of living bodies but the care of symbolic bodies – that means all of the post-mortal documents, texts, images and objects related to the lives of the great negators. The collection and preservation of these symbolic

---

10 Friedrich Nietzsche, *Untimely Meditations*, ed. Daniel Breazeale, trans. R. J. Hollingdale, Cambridge: Cambridge University Press, 1997, p. 69.

bodies is impossible without institutions of public care such as cemeteries, libraries and museums. Writing his historical narrative, Hegel almost automatically relied on the already established difference between historically relevant and irrelevant symbolic bodies – a difference that was produced by these institutions. Nietzsche understands history in a similar way. His hope that his *Zarathustra* will be read and studied in the distant future demonstrates the unshakable and, one should admit, naïve belief in such institutions of public care.

In fact, Nietzsche was, as a living body, perfectly decadent – weak and often ill. So he understood not merely his own living body as an explosive, healthy body but, rather, this body extended by the body of his texts. Not accidentally, he included the descriptions of his books in his self-description in *Ecce Homo*. Nietzsche cared for the health of his own body with the goal of letting this body produce especially explosive and, thus, healthy books. Speaking about his book on Zarathustra, Nietzsche uses the same image as Socrates – the image of giving birth. Half-ironically, and obviously referring to *Theaetetus,* Nietzsche writes that he was pregnant with *Zarathustra* for eighteen months: 'This period of exactly eighteen months, might suggest, at least to Buddhists, that I am in reality a female elephant.'[11] However, Nietzsche gives birth not to a human (or even elephant) child and also not to the truth but, rather, to the figure of the *Übermensch*. This figure is – or, at least, should be – representative of the future for the whole of humanity. The *Übermensch* takes on mortal risk not for the sake of an idea but because he is, so to say, *überhealthy*, and thus an embodiment of the will to power. Health means dynamics, energy, aggressiveness. 'True health' cannot be reached because there is no perfect, final 'state of health' but rather a permanent flow of energy that cannot stop itself. That means that history cannot come to an end. The flow of energy flows always further – and thus produces ever new negations/creations through *überhealthy*, explosive personalities similar to Zarathustra.

But *Zarathustra* is, of course, not (yet) a real, living body but rather the body of a book. The content of a book can be healthy and

11 Nietzsche, *Ecce Homo*, p. 97.

explosive but a book as a particular material object still should be cared for – written, edited, published, kept in libraries and taught at universities. The figure of the *Übermensch* can become a monogram for the future humankind only as an object of the institutional care. Vital energy thus seems to be only a means to enact historical deeds and produce works that could find their way into historical annals. Or, in other words, the explosion of healthy energy is used here to produce a new symbolic body that could take a prestigious place among other symbolic bodies inside the general system of care. After the death of God and the loss of faith in the immortality of the soul, the artificial, bureaucratically administered symbolic body becomes the only form of the after-life that we can imagine. The *Übermensch* rejects the social care in the name of great health – he wants to live dangerously and is ready to give up the desire of self-preservation. Thus, at the first glance, the *Übermensch* seems to practice self-care as struggle against the biopolitical state that makes its population sick by turning it into a mass of patients. However, in reality the *Übermensch* still relies on the institutional care of symbolic bodies. The surplus of health, the *überhealth*, is a promise of *über-survival*, of after-life as a book, an artwork, as a memory of an extraordinary historic action. Nietzschean great health is a desire for recognition and fame and thus can be re-inscribed into the Hegelian historical narrative. It is what Alexandre Kojève did in his Introduction to Hegel's *Phenomenology of the Spirit* – a series of lectures that he delivered in Paris in 1933–9.

4

The Sage as Caretaker

In his lectures on Hegel, Kojève claimed to be simply repeating the course of Hegel's thought in a different language (French) and in a different historical context. In fact, Kojève's philosophical approach is more Nietzschean than Hegelian. Kojève is interested in history and primarily in political history. But for him, history is moved not by reason nor by humanity's search for freedom but by the individual's desire for public recognition, According to Kojève we can speak of desire of the first and second orders.

Desire of the first order signals to us our existence in the world. It is quite a reversal of our standard understanding of the word 'desire'. Usually, desire is interpreted as leading to the attachment to the things of this world. That is why, since Plato, philosophy and religion have tried to isolate the human soul from corporeal desires and direct it towards the contemplation of itself. However, today we are attached to the world not primarily through desires but through science. Modern contemplation is contemplation of the world – and not of an Idea or of God. For us, it is therefore not the rejection of desires that opens the way to self-consciousness but, on the contrary, the emergence of desire. It is desire that isolates and opposes us to the world: 'The man who contemplates is "absorbed" by what he contemplates; the "knowing subject" "loses" himself in the object that is known . . . The man who is "absorbed" in that he is contemplating can be "brought back to himself" only by a Desire; by the desire to eat, for example . . . The (human) I is the I of . . . Desire'.[1] Desire turns one from contemplation to action. This action is always 'negation'. The I of Desire is emptiness that consumes, negates and destroys everything 'external', 'given'.

---

1 Alexandre Kojève, *Introduction to the Reading of Hegel: Lectures on the Phenomenology of Spirit*, ed. Allan Bloom, trans. James H. Nichols Jr., Ithaca, NY: Cornell University Press, 1980, pp. 3–4.

But desire of the first order produces only Self-Sentiment and not yet Self-Consciousness. Self-Consciousness is produced by a specific type of desire – the 'anthropogenic' desire that is desire not of particular things but desire of the desire of the other: 'Thus, in the relationship between man and woman, for example, Desire is human only if the one desires not the body but desire of the other'. Here, desire becomes dialectical. Anthropogenic desire is the negation of animal desire – a negation of the negation. It is this anthropogenic desire that initiates and moves history: 'human history is history of desired Desires . . . Self-Consciousness, the human reality . . . is, finally, a function of Desire for recognition.'[2] Here Kojève refers to an initial battle of Self-Consciousnesses that is described by Hegel in his *Phenomenology*. Two Self-Consciousnesses fight each other – and one of them wins the battle. Then the other self-consciousness has two choices: (1) to die, or (2) to survive and work to satisfy the desire of the winner. Thus, we see two types of humans emerge: masters and slaves. The masters prefer to die rather than work for other masters – and the slaves accept work as their fate. Only the desires of the master are recognized. The slave supresses his or her own desires to satisfy the desire of the master. The work that the slave does is alienated work that finds no social recognition. On its surface, history is the history of the masters. They fight against each other to achieve recognition and fame. When a master wins a battle he uses his position as a winner to satisfy his personal desires. At the same time, the master becomes more and more dependent on the slaves who, through their work, transform the world in which the master lives – so that, in the end, the master becomes a prisoner of a world controlled by the work of others, by the work of the slaves.

Of course, Kojève was very much influenced by Marx and his understanding of class struggle as the motor of history. However, according to Kojève classes constitute themselves not through their relation to the process of production but through their relation to direct violence and political power. The 'masters' are ready to fight for

---

2 Ibid., pp. 6, 7.

the recognition of their desires and to die in battle. The 'slaves' prefer to live in peace – and thus are condemned to work for the masters. This work is understood as a work of care: the slaves work to satisfy the desires of upper class, to care for the well-being of the upper class.

But what about the philosopher? Philosophers are similar to masters because they are moved by the desire for recognition, but at the same time philosophers seek recognition not through the fight for their personal interests and desires but by offering the public new ideas about the organization of society and the common good. The philosophers can and should govern the state – here Kojève is in agreement with Plato. But Kojève does not believe that a master, a king, a tyrant can be taught to rule according to philosophical principles. Rather, the philosopher has to take power through revolution and become a philosopher-tyrant. Indeed, for Kojève, the philosopher is not merely somebody who writes philosophical books and reflects on historical events, including the end of history. On the contrary, the philosopher is an activist who struggles to change history – and the end of history is precisely the moment at which the philosopher takes power. Philosophy thus comes not after the event, as with Hegel's owl of wisdom, but precedes and produces historical events. The philosopher has to cease to be contemplative and become creative and violent – here, one can see the double influence of Marx and Nietzsche. However, Kojève distrusts the willingness to serve the common good as the sole motivation of revolutionary action. Philosophers act historically because they are motivated by the desire of desire – by the promise of recognition.

For Kojève, Socrates is also primarily motivated by the desire for recognition – like the Sophists.[3] Kojeve does not believe that the people can be persuaded by 'rational' discourses, because all the discourses sound more or less rational. The listeners and readers are rather seduced by philosophical ideas that sound not rational but

3 Alexandre Kojève, in Leo Strauss, *On Tyranny: Corrected and Expanded Edition, Including the Strauss–Kojève Correspondence*, ed. Victor Gourevitch and Michael S. Roth, Chicago: University of Chicago Press, 2013, p. 261.

crazy, unheard of, 'creative'. They follow a philosopher rather than his or her ideas. In different places in his writings, Kojève insists that it is the followers who create the conditions for a crazy philosopher to be recognized and thus become a rational philosopher.[4] Only when philosophers gain a substantial following can their ideas begin to be recognized as reasonable and serious enough. That means that being rational is not an original characteristic of a particular philosophical discourse but an effect of recognition, a sign of its popular success. In this respect, Kojève is the best theoretician of the contemporary age in which the importance of ideas is measured by the number of people who share them, or at least who like them.

Philosophers achieve ultimate success not when they lead followers to the contemplation of truth but when they become revolutionary leaders and then rulers of post-revolutionary states. The philosophical, post-revolutionary state ends history because it transcends the division of humanity into masters and slaves. The philosopher is not a traditional master, but he is also not a slave. Unlike the traditional master, the philosopher-ruler works – but he works to transform the society according to his own ideas and plans. In other words, the end of history is marked by the emergence of the figure of the working master. For Kojève, such a working tyrant was Stalin. That is why he believed that it was Stalin and not Napoleon, as Hegel believed, who ended the history of revolutions and wars.[5] The Soviet Union was, for Kojève, not only the workers' state but also a working state. Here the history of the class struggle seemed, indeed, to come to an end.

So Kojève is half-Nietzschean, half-Hegelian. On the one hand, he interprets history as a history of the will to power – of the struggle for recognition and prestige. In this respect, Kojève is very close to Nietzsche. On the other hand, he wants the philosopher to become not merely famous and celebrated but the true master, the ruler as

---

4 Kojève, *On Tyranny and Wisdom*, in Strauss, *On Tyranny*, pp. 172ff.

5 Alexandre Kojève, *The Notion of Authority: A Brief Presentation*, trans. Hager Weslati, London and New York: Verso, 2014. Originally published as *La notion de l'Autorité*, Paris: Gallimard, 2004.

well as the worker. As a working ruler, the philosopher should offer to society ideas that society will be ready to share and the realization of which it would be ready to participate in. And it is, of course, a very non-Nietzschean conception of the ruler. Nietzsche did not believe in ideas that could be shared. He was interested in admirers but not in followers – whereas for Kojève the problem of the following is central. In his book on the notion of authority,[6] Kojève develops a theory of personal power based on popularity and not on the traditional mechanisms of repression or democratic mechanisms of representation. From the contemporary point of view, this theory is a theory of what we call now 'populism'. However, Kojève believed that populism belonged to the historical past, to the era of wars and revolutions. The future belongs instead to post-political administration. And administration does not fight but engages in care.

After the end of history, the struggle for recognition loses its historical relevance. Kojève defines the post-historical state as 'universal and homogeneous'. In this state everybody is recognized to the same degree – and, thus, the desire of recognition is fully satisfied. For the philosophers, it means that they can be recognized merely as famous authors by the 'republic of letters'. Such recognition is flattering, but it does not change the real conditions of social and political life. True philosophers, after they win political power, cease to fight for recognition and become Sages. The Sage is a caretaker of the post-historical population that has lost its historical ambitions and with them its true humanity. The Sage protects this humanity by preventing it from slipping back into history with all its violence and suffering. Basically, this population is interested only in consumption – in the satisfaction of their animal desires – and thus has lost the ability of critique and reflection. In the first version of his famous footnote to his *Introduction*,[7] Kojève asserts that, after the end of history, man ceases to be opposed to Nature because the desire for recognition, which opposed man to Nature, is satisfied. Here Kojève refers to

6 Kojève, 'Introduction', *Notion of Authority*, pp. 158–62.

7 Ibid., p. 159.

Marx, who predicted that the historical Realm of Necessity, which placed humanity in opposition to Nature and one class in opposition to another class, will be replaced by the Realm of Freedom, which will open to humanity the possibility of enjoying 'art, love, play etc.' in harmony with Nature.[8]

However, Kojève later realized that this idyllic vision implies, among other things, that the post-historical population would lose its historical memory – and even the knowledge of its own post-historicity. In an extension of a footnote written for the second edition of his *Introduction to the Reading of Hegel*, Kojève accepts his previous error and concedes that the disappearance of historical man also renders traditional notions of art, love and play obsolete: 'Hence it would have to be admitted that after the end of history men would construct their edifices and works of art as birds build their nests and spiders spin their webs, would perform their musical concerts after the fashion of frogs and cicadas, would play like young animals and would indulge in love like adult beasts'.[9] But most important, the human animal would lose language, which is the only medium of Wisdom. 'Animals of the species Homo sapiens will react by conditioned reflexes to vocal signals . . . What would disappear . . . is not only Philosophy or the search for discursive Wisdom, but also that Wisdom itself. For in these post-historical animals, there would no longer be any understanding of the World and of self'.[10] One can say that the post-historical population is a population of masters or, in other words, of consumers who work only in so far that their work allows them to consume.

Only the Sage remains uninterested in consumption. He continues working – and he works for nothing. One can say that the Sage is a perfect machine that works beyond desire – because his desire is already satisfied. For Kojève, the fact that the Sage works is more important than the goal of his work. Work becomes an

---

8 Ibid.
9 Ibid.
10 Ibid., p. 160.

attribute of power instead of being the fate of the slave. And what is even more important is that it is not creative work. The Sage is not a creative genius but a universal caretaker. And the work of the caretaker is, as it was said, a monotonous, repetitive and in this sense eternal work. The Sage is immortal as a machine is immortal. Indeed, every machine can be well maintained and repaired for a very long time. When a machine is broken or worn out beyond repair, it can be replaced by exactly the same machine performing the same functions. The machine is immortal because it is infinitely substitutable. The Sage is also infinitely substitutable because every Sage embodies the same wisdom – the same historical memory. The Sage is a permanently working machine of discourse and care. If the Sage realizes a Nietzschean dream, it is not a dream of great health but that of the eternal return of the same. The emergence of the Sage signals the transcending of the opposition between care and self-care. The Sage is not interested in the future, post-mortal fame. He finds satisfaction in the anonymous work of care. It is precisely this anonymity that guarantees that the work of care will be continued in the future – so that the Sage experiences his life as having an infinite perspective.

There is an important shift from the Hegelian to Kojevian perspective – a shift caused primarily by the influence of Marx. The opposition between spirit and body becomes an opposition between the human as machine and the human as animal. Accordingly, the notion of health becomes ambivalent. A man as a machine is considered healthy when he is working, when he is functional. The system of care has the goal of keeping people in good health to enable them to continue working. When an individual falls ill or dies, it ceases to work and is replaced by a similar individual who is able to perform the same work. In this sense, man as a worker is potentially immortal.

However, in the case of man as an animal, the situation is different. The animal has desires. Even domesticated, working animals have desires. When an animal experiences desire, it ceases to work – and tries to satisfy that desire. This means that having a desire is unhealthy. In relationship to work, having a desire means the same thing as falling ill or even dying. That is why, in the framework of technologically driven civilization, animal desires are suppressed or at least drastically reduced. But for an animal to have desires and to realize them is healthy – and to suppress them is unhealthy. One can argue that the suppression of desires can save the individual – helping it to live longer. For man as an animal, however, longevity and survival are not the supreme values. The individual knows that it is going to die anyway. And it knows that, as an animal, it is not substitutable. Of course, all animals are included in the chain of births and deaths: here, the species dominates over the individual. But in case of humans, the set of desires is often individual and unrepeatable. Self-care thus begins again to contradict the system of care – because the system of care cares for a human as a worker and not for the human as an animal. Health begins to be understood as the intensity of desire – as the ability of the desiring human to break out of the system of care and fight for the satisfaction of his or her desires up to the bitter end. Nietzschean desire of future recognition can be transcended by the desire of anonymous repetition of the same. But the explosion of the vital forces in man belongs to a different, non-historical order and cannot be historicized. If the Sage has become a worker, the animal in man has remained a master.

5

The Sovereign Animal

In his philosophical texts written after World War II, Bataille repeats the Nietzschean protest – but this time not against Hegelian historical reason but against the dominance of work. Desire interrupts the working process just as it interrupts the process of contemplation. To use the same Kojevian example, the desire for food and other bodily, animal desires produces self-sentiment – and that turns the attention of the worker from the working process to his or her own body. Let us imagine that a machine functioned in the same way. Machines are powered, after all, not by some mystical flows of energy but by the supply of oil or electricity. Let us imagine that if this supply were switched off, the machines experienced the desire for oil or electricity and tried to renew their supply – like a worker would do looking for food. In this case, the machines will indeed be behaving like animals. Desire would cause them to care for their own survival and well-being. However, that is not what happens to machines as we know them. Machines do not worry about their survival. But animals and humans do.

For Bataille, a desire to renew one's own energy to be able to continue to work is not sufficient. He is interested in a desire that would totally defunctionalize us. As a former student of Kojève, Bataille thinks in terms of the original opposition between masters and slaves. Kojève had argued that if, having lost the struggle for recognition, you preferred to die rather than to work for the winner, you will remain a master. A glorious death makes one a master no less than victory. For Bataille, victory in the battle for recognition became impossible after the collapse of the *ancien régime* and the democratization of society. But the option of glorious self-destruction remained. The rejection of work can be seen as a sign of weakness, of illness, of lack of strength and discipline. In this case, the workers remain inside the system of social control that either tries to restore their capacity to work or to put them under the care of the institutions of welfare. But one can reject the work because one has a surplus of energy, of vital forces that cannot be absorbed by the working process. This surplus of energy pushes one towards revolt against the routine of work and the system of care.

Nietzsche believed that this surplus of energy had to come from within one's own body if this body is endowed by great health. But according to Bataille, that surplus of energy comes from outside – from the cosmic energy circulating on the surface of the Earth.[1] Cosmic energies are understood here as the ultimate caretaker of earthly life – the caretaker who expends the energy that makes this life possible. However, the cosmos is a too magnanimous caretaker. It sends too much energy to Earth – so that not all of this energy can be absorbed and exhausted through work. The surplus of energy – the 'accursed share', as Bataille calls it – can and should be spent, not through the working process alone, but rather through destruction and self-destruction. Great health thus becomes a kind of infection by the additional influx of nonhuman vital energies. The Nietzschean difference between great health and decadence disappears: both of them become the manifestations of excess, including excessive consumption and unproductive waste of energy. Bataille develops the discourse on 'general economy' – the economic theory that takes into consideration not only work, production and accumulation but also consumption, luxury and waste. Now, Bataille was, of course, not the first author who tried to expand the field of economy by including in it the value produced not only by work and accumulation but also that by loss and destruction.

Bataille's theory of general economy is heavily dependent on Marcel Mauss's theory of symbolic exchange, which he developed in his essay *The Gift*.[2] Even if, at first glance, Mauss's essay focuses on the description and analysis of gift exchange in so-called primitive

---

1 Georges Bataille, *The Accursed Share*, vol. 1, New York, Zone Books, 1991, pp. 21–22.

2 Marcel Mauss, *The Gift : Forms and Functions of Exchange in Archaic Societies*, trans. Ian Gunnison, London: Cohen & West, 1966, p. 14.

cultures, its actual goal is to show that the logic of symbolic exchange continues to operate in the modern age. For example, in our society we feel the obligation to reciprocate when we receive a gift. When we are not able to do so, we accept that the giver has a higher social status than we have. For the giver, the gift is a loss but also a form of an attack against the recipient. The counter-gift is a counter-attack. That is true as well for religious sacrifice or charity: a more generous giver is accorded higher social status. Gift-giving is thus a form of aggression, a manifestation of the will to power. It is important to see that the value of the gift has nothing to do with the usefulness of this gift for its recipient. The act of giving has its own symbolic value, which is recognized by society in an obligatory way.

The crucial confirmation of this thesis is the custom of potlatch, which was practised especially by the Indian nations of North America but can also be found across the world. Potlatch is a competition in the destruction of one's own wealth: the competing tribes burn their houses and fields, kill domestic animals and slaves. The tribe that has destroyed the most wealth gets the highest rank for the period until the new potlatch.[3] Mauss describes the laws of symbolic exchange of gifts to which all societies, including modern societies are subject. However, by the word 'law' Mauss understands a certain social convention – even if he believes that this convention has a universal validity and governs the totality of the economy, of which the monetary economy, or the market, is only a part. Bataille, on the contrary, interprets the laws of the symbolic economy as quasi-natural laws from which humans cannot escape.

Indeed, the amount of energy sent by the Sun can be considered as a gift to mankind that should be reciprocated. However, humanity is unable to reciprocate – to create a counter-gift that could be given to the Sun. Icarus tried it and failed. So potlatch is the only answer: humans practise (self)-destruction to balance the excess of energy that they have gotten from the Sun. As I have already noted, humans are in any case doomed: even if they do not voluntarily and gloriously

---

3 Ibid., p. 95.

destroy their own wealth, it is destroyed catastrophically – through economic crisis, wars and revolutions. In other words, the Sun does not allow human history to end. By sending more energy than can be absorbed by peaceful work, the Sun provokes the violence and counter-violence that keep history moving forward. This movement has no goal, but it has a cause. This cause is not only the gift of the Sun but also the ambitions of the individuals who want to be sovereign and recognized as such by society. These individuals prefer to spend their lives in a glorious way and become the subjects of potlatch with the Sun, instead of becoming its passive victims.

Bataille sees bourgeois society as a society of confusion. On the one hand, this society respects the work and effort that one engages in to achieve greater wealth and higher social rank. However, bourgeois society is still living culturally in the shadow of its feudal, sovereign-tist past. The bourgeois subject is half-animal and half-machine. Bataille's concept of sovereignty is also contradictory. On the one hand, following Kojève, he expects from Communism the establishment of a new sovereignty – the sovereignty of work. Thus, he writes: 'Today, sovereignty is no longer alive except in the perspective of Communism',[4] where it takes form of the 'sovereign renunciation of sovereignty'.[5] Here, Stalin is again paradigmatic for this new kind of sovereignty because he denies himself pleasure, leisure and satisfaction of his personal desires in the name of serving the idea of Communism.[6] Communist sovereignty is the sovereignty of a man who decided to become a machine – to reject the animal half of human nature.

But Bataille calls Communist sovereignty 'negative sovereignty'. He obviously prefers the opposite, positive option to achieving sovereignty: to reject work. When man rejects work, he ceases to be a machine and becomes an animal, a beast. Sovereignty equals animality: 'The sovereign man lives and dies as an animal. But he is a

4 Bataille, *Accursed Share*, vol. 2/3, p. 261.
5 Ibid., p. 322.
6 Ibid., p. 321f.

man nevertheless'.[7] It is the old feudal sovereignty but totally de-Christianized. In the real, pre-bourgeois Christian world, even a king was a slave of God. But Bataille imagines the feudal lord as headless, as *acéphale* (to use the title of the famous magazine that Bataille edited from 1936 to 1939) manifesting anonymous, 'nameless' vital *überforces*. It is appropriate that Bataille's grave has no name on it. It is to be found in the cemetery in Vézelay under a hill on the top of which one can admire a majestic cathedral that marks the place where the Second and Third Crusades started.

Bataille often speaks about death and does so in very materialistic terms – for him, death is not nothingness but a decomposing cadaver. This cadaver, together with sexuality, defecation, urinating, vomiting and other body functions, presents the other of the 'normal body' that is formed and regulated by our civilization as a mere tool used for doing a certain kind of work.[8] In this sense, death is the main proof that we are not merely working tools. Desire for sovereignty turns passive dying into active killing. The sovereign is a killer. Bataille writes about the natural death that one passively waits for:

> But beyond this passive negation, active rebellion is easy and is bound to occur in the end: he whom the world of utility tended to reduce to the state of a thing not subject to death, hence not subject to killing, ultimately demands the violation of the prohibition that he had accepted. Then, by killing, he escapes the subordination that he refuses, and he violently rids himself of the aspect of a tool or a thing, which he had assumed only for a time. At this price, sovereign existence is restored to him, the sovereign moment that *alone* finally justifies a conditional and temporary submission to necessity . . . If the sovereign, or sacred, world that stands against the world of practice is indeed the domain of death, it is not that of faintheartedness. From the viewpoint of the sovereign man, faintheartedness and the

7 Ibid., p. 219.

8 *The Bataille Reader*, ed. Fred Botting and Scott Wilson, Oxford: Blackwell, 1997, p. 149.

> fearful representation of death belong to the world of practice, that is, of subordination. In fact, subordination is always rooted in necessity; subordination is always grounded in the alleged need to avoid death.[9]

There is no doubt that Bataille identified here the main aspect of modern and contemporary culture. The main hero of this culture is a criminal, a murderer. The crime story is the only contemporary narrative that is able to capture the collective imagination. Be it a novel or a film, it must be a crime story to have real commercial success. Under the rule of law, the sovereign (the king of the *ancien régime*) becomes an outlaw. The outlaw is truly sovereign and even sacred because he or she represents not (ordinary) life but death in a society for which death is the absolute master. However, to represent death means not to use death for any practical purpose: the sovereign and sacral are defined by Bataille in opposition to utility. One should therefore kill only to become unlawful – and not to achieve any particular goals that would resituate the killer in the profane world of utility. Of course, such killers who kill only to become sovereign and maybe even sacral are rare (mostly to be found in Dostoyevsky's novels). In the majority of crime stories, the killers have practical goals, such as getting money or revenge. However, their sovereignty is usually saved by the authors because the killers mostly fail to reach their goal and are thus saved from the danger of becoming ordinary. But what does this opposition between the utilitarian and the sovereign, or between machine and animal, say about our health? It seems that both of the members of this opposition make us unhealthy. Work is exhausting and depressive. Killing cannot be described as perfectly healthy. The occasional encounter with decomposing corpses, shitting and vomiting can lead to further infections. However, infection ceases to function here in strict opposition to health. Indeed, at the moment at which great health begins to be understood as an infection, as an influx of stimulating and, at the same time, destructive energy,

9 Ibid., p. 318.

infection becomes recognized as a source of creativity. One has to be infected to become creative. In contemporary society with its cult of creativity, self-care easily takes the form of self-infection, including the use of drugs. One should not forget that the use of drugs was, for example, an integral part of the Aztec sacral rituals that so fascinated Bataille.

The infection of which we are speaking now is, thus, less biological than cultural infection. The society of care keeps memory of the ancient habits, rituals and customs. These rituals and habits do not necessarily fit into the rationalized modern and contemporary way of life. That creates the state of confusion of which Bataille speaks and opens the possibility of revivals and re-enactments of the past. As it was already mentioned, the will to excess and hazardous self-destruction can be explained not only through a revolt of the animal in man but also through imitation of the pre-modern patterns of behaviour that survived in the texture of the modern social life. These patterns become also known through historical chronicles and anthropological research. That demonstrates that putting at risk one's own health should not necessarily be explained as an attack of the vital energies and forces against the dominating culture. Rather, the conflict between aggressive self-assertion and institutional care is the fundamental characteristic of this culture itself. Everybody is caught in the middle of this conflict and has to take sides – or to try to find a middle way between them.

6

The Infectious Sacred

In his book *Man and the Sacred*, Roger Caillois treats the sacred and the infectious as synonymous. He writes that in Rome, the word *sacer* meant that 'which cannot be touched without defilement'.[1] The traditional social order differentiated between the profane space of regular practical life and the sacred space in which the forces of the magical and miraculous reigned. Unregulated contact between the profane and the sacred could lead to making both of them impure. The sacral is fascinating and dangerous at the same time. And the sacred has nothing to do with any moral distinction between good and evil. 'The *fascinans* corresponds to the intoxicating qualities of the sacred, of the Dionysian giddiness, the ecstasy, the unity of transport ... Analogously, the demonic, at the opposite pole of the sacred and sharing its terrible and dangerous characteristics, excites in its turn equally irrational sentiments that are opposed to one's self-interest'.[2] This is why in traditional cultures the profane subject had to take all possible precautions, including fasting or ritual bathing, in order to prevent infection through contact with the sacred.

The same cultures strictly regulate the relationship between the sexes, as well as between masters and servants. Caillois stresses the fact that, in traditional cultures, relationships of power are generally accepted as self-evident: 'Whatever the kind of power – civil, military, or religious – it is only a consequence of consent.'[3] Of course, these relationships change, not as a result of a better insight, critical analysis or rational social reform, but rather as a slow but inescapable loss of energy that lets the old order collapse.[4] This collapse weakens

1 Roger Caillois, *Man and the Sacred*, trans. Meyer Barash, Champaign: University of Illinois Press, 1959, p. 36.

2 Ibid., pp. 37–8.

3 Ibid., p. 90.

4 Ibid., p. 96.

mechanisms of protection and leads to the massive infusion of sacred energies into society. The influx of sacral energies takes a form of total infection and intoxication that plunges society into chaos. Work stops, ecstasy begins. Chaos reigns. Society comes back to point zero, to its initial starting point. As a result, society becomes reinvigorated through 'creative vigor' and the 'fountain of youth': 'the re-enactment of the creative period' starts.'[5] 'The ritual of creation that has been handed down, and which alone is capable of leading to success, is repeated. Actors imitate the heroic deeds and gestures. They wear masks that identify them with this ancestor.'[6] Profane work is understood here as a manifestation of the passive mode of existence dictated by wisdom, by fear of death, by timidity and contemplation. The sacred, on the other hand, is audacious and creative: 'Such an antagonism between wisdom and audacity, of the desire for rest and the spirit of adventure, seems like the aspect of collective existence that is most obviously reflected in the way in which the individual interprets the sacred.'[7]

This passage that refers to Nietzsche's celebration of audacity and adventure shows that Caillois, similar to Mauss, is much less interested in traditional cultures than in his own culture – and especially in the choice between regular work, on the one hand, and festival, violence and war, on the other hand. For Caillois, the Enlightenment and the domination of scientific thinking over modern societies did not abolish the sacred but rather let the sacred infect these societies through deep dissatisfaction: 'Stability is no longer regarded as the highest good, nor are moderation, prudence, or conformity to established usage regarded as among the highest virtues. Security, comfort, a good reputation, and honor are no longer deemed as most desirable advantages.'[8] The modern individual loses its patience, it can no more live a life that is reduced to waiting for natural death. Thus, put in a situation of a choice between the sacral flame and profane putrefaction,

5 Ibid., p. 107.
6 Ibid., p. 108.
7 Ibid., p. 125.
8 Ibid., p. 136.

it chooses the flame. And this is not only an individual but also a collective choice. In modernity, the sacred becomes not only internalized by individuals who are unhappy with the tediousness of their lives but also produces the phenomenon of modern war. Like the ancient sacral festival, war is a manifestation of the fury of destruction that embraces the whole of the society. However, if the traditional festival kept the balance between destruction and regeneration, modern war is able to release the forces of destruction that can destroy the whole of the humanity. At the end of the book, Caillois discusses the possibility that life as such will be ended by the coming total war. The only way to avoid it seems to be a return to the old system of rules and rituals that protected the profane sphere from deadly infection through the sacred. Bataille's and Caillois's texts are, in many ways, similar. But while Bataille calls for a meeting with the ultimate Other manifesting itself as a decomposing corpse, Caillois advises us to subject this meeting to certain protective measures – in order to avoid total infection and the death of everything living.

7

The People as Caretaker

In different ways, all the authors discussed earlier were searching for a direct, unmediated access to the totality of the world, the Universe, Being. Indeed, if I have a direct, unmediated access to the powers and forces that govern the whole of the world, I lose my dependence on the institutions of care – and can practice self-care. After all, these institutions represent only a small part of the world, of the Universe. Thus, I can take up a metaposition towards them and judge their activities instead of being judged by them. In other words, I can judge knowledge from the position of non-knowledge.

To move beyond the institutional framework of care is seductive because it offers the promise of being relieved from work and thus becoming truly healthy. Indeed, living inside the institutions of care means also working for them. And working for them means not only practising one's profession but also investing a lot of effort to build a career, to get more access and power inside institutional hierarchies. It is an exhausting type of work. In this sense, the search for the metaposition is intimately connected with the search for better health. But to what degree have the different strategies for this ontological search proven to be good for our health? In a somewhat paradoxical manner, one can say that the most favourable for our health is the Platonic ontology of reason. Indeed, the contemplation of Logos has no urgency, produces no time pressure, no stress, no hysteria related to the window of opportunity that is always in danger of closing in the next moment. And it is precisely this sense of urgency that is bad for our heart, metabolism and vascular system in the first place.

Of course, Platonism and then Christianity and Buddhism were accused of being disdainful and disrespectful towards the body and its needs and desires. However, one has the impression that Christian and Buddhist monks were in relatively good health. The situation changed when the contemplation of truth was replaced by mobilization for creative work. Not eternity but the future became the privileged meta-institutional place. The individual was supposed to break all the institutional rules, to undermine all the traditional conventions and in doing so, to create something radically new. It was not clear – and could not be clear by definition – what this new should be, but it had to be different from anything that had come before. Hegel understood the work of progress as the work of negation. In the framework of Hegel's dialectical logic the new emerged as a side effect of the negation of the old and not as a goal in itself. Thus, the production of the new had to end with the negation of the negation – with the end of history.

This is why Nietzsche proposed the will to power as the perpetual motor of progress. The will to power produces not negations but rather differences, new possibilities of human existence. According to Nietzsche, the will to power is an adventure – sailing into the open sea of the unknown. Thus, the will to power becomes able to judge known history from the perspective of the unknown future that this will is about to create. As Deleuze rightly says in his book on Nietzsche: 'New values derive from affirmation: values which were unknown up to the present, that is to say up to the moment when the legislator takes the place of the "scholar", *creation takes the place of knowledge itself* and affirmation takes the place of all negations.'[1]

But what happens to our bodies as a consequence of their mobilization through the will to power? Of course, the new, creative man, or better, the *Übermensch*, is supposed to have the 'great health' that allows him to go through all difficulties while keeping his health intact. However, the average person has this kind of health only for a short period of time – during his or her young years. The celebration of desire, will to power and vital energies leads to the celebration of youth. But youth is short – the future is not a creative adventure but the illnesses of old age. The vitalistic discourse of affirmation transforms history into the eternal return of generational change. The

---

1 Gilles Deleuze, *Nietzsche and Philosophy*, trans. Hugh Tomlinson, New York: Athlone Press/Continuum, 1983, p. 173.]

creative projects that inspired one generation become abandoned and forgotten by the next one. As a result, all these projects remain unrealized. Of course, different generations live different lives. But they become different not because of the affirmative will to difference that internally mobilizes the bodies of these generations. In fact, every new generation merely accommodates its lifestyle to the dominant technological conditions. Change emerges not within individuals but is imposed on them by technological developments.

Work produces new technology and thus transforms the world in which we live. The world is transformed more by the work of slaves than the political struggles of the masters. At the end of history, the masters become totally imprisoned by the world built for them by the slaves – by the world of industry. That is why the Nietzschean will to power stages a revolt of masters against the domination of slave mentality and morality. The will to power migrates from the present into the future. The former masters become the creatives who master the future – being unable to master the present. They create the symbolic bodies that are designed to survive thousands of years – not unlike the Egyptian pyramids. That is the main difference between the creatives and ordinary workers who work to live and live to work. The creatives, on the contrary, are interested more in the after-life than in this life. That is the actual origin of the idea of 'great health'. The creative needs great health in order to make a surplus effort in comparison with the ordinary worker, to mobilize the additional energy of Sun, ancient magic and ecstatic forces to project them into the future. However, even an *Übermensch* cannot control the future. It is instead controlled by state institutions and big corporations – with their long-term investments and planning. The individual cannot compete with these monsters without causing serious damage to its health. Thus, in terms of health, the future does not look like a good substitute for eternity.

In this respect, it is interesting to look more closely at Bataille's and Caillois's discourses. On the one hand, they sound perfectly Nietzschean – evoking and celebrating the Dionysian forces, festive intoxication, the surge of the vital forces. On the other hand, both authors are obviously not futuristic but instead nostalgic. They do not so much preach the future adventures as they admire the vestiges and traces of ancient cultural formations that have survived historical change and remain present within modern culture. Characteristically, the festivals are described by Caillois as only imitating, re-enacting, the original explosion of creative energies. Their protagonists carry the masks of the dead ancestors – merely performing their roles. Every repetition of these rituals is a repetition of the repetition, imitation of the imitation, re-enactment of the re-enactment. Nevertheless – or, rather, precisely because of that – these rituals seem to revitalize their participants. Indeed, if some life forms have survived the transition from the past to the present they seem to be able to survive also the transition from the present to the future. Here the search for true health shifts from belief in the vital forces to interest in the survival of the past in the present – as the promise of the survival of the present in the future. In other words, to interest in the modern institution of care that make such a survival possible.

Caillois develops this interest in his later theory of games. The game is the ancient sacred ritual that has survived its mythical past and now functions as recreation. Caillois states that the majority of games include the aspect of competition: 'Competition is a law of modem life.'[2] However, through the game the competition becomes a spectacle: 'I have already had occasion to stress that every competition is also a spectacle. It unfolds according to identical rules, and with the same anticipation of the outcome. It requires the presence of an audience which crowds about the ticket windows of the stadium or velodrome just as at those of the theater and cinema.'[3] The society of competition is at the same time a society of the spectacle.

Since the appearance of the famous book by Guy Debord, the spectacle has often been criticized for producing masses of passive spectators. What is overlooked by this criticism is that the position of

---

2 Roger Caillois, *Man, Play and Games*, trans. Meyer Barash, Urbana and Chicago: University of Illinois Press, 2001 [1961].

3 Ibid., p. 74.

the spectator is restful, healthy for somebody who is exploited and exhausted through the permanent competition 'in real life'. The spectacle of competition allows one to take up a metaposition in relation to it – similar to the position of Socrates looking at the competitions of the Sophists. In fact, Debord is very Socratic in his double strategy: to contemplate the spectacle and to formulate a critical position towards the spectacle. However, as soon as one begins to formulate a critical position towards the spectacle one becomes 'spectacular' – transposed from the audience to the stage, positioned as one competitor among others. Socrates becomes a 'Sophist', Debord becomes an 'artist'. That is why Debord struggled against 'spectacularity' – not so much to abandon the position of the spectator as to avoid being judged according to the rule of competition. Notwithstanding his critique of the passivity of the spectator, Debord preferred a position in the audience to a position on the stage. The spectacle of 'great health' is an imitation of the moment of creation – but precisely because of that it reveals the original act of creation itself as being nothing more than a mere theatrical effect.

The same can be said about games of chance, like roulette or a lottery, that let us contemplate our dependence on fate. Indeed, Caillois asserts that almost every form of competition is experienced by its participants as unfair. In our society, the rules of meritocratic competition try to compensate for the privileges that are related to birth, like the wealth and social position of the family and access to education. However, these rules are never experienced as sufficient. Caillois writes: 'Under these conditions, *alea* seems a necessary compensation for *agōn*, and its natural complement . . . Recourse to chance helps people tolerate competition that is unfair or too rugged. At the same time, it leaves hope in the dispossessed that free competition is still possible in the lowly stations in life, which are necessarily more numerous.'[4] Here, the confrontation with fate does not lead to tragedy – at least, when the player does not become obsessed with the play. However, the event of catharsis is still restaged and experienced

4 Ibid., p. 115.

by the players and audience – even if the antique belief in fate has been lost.

The border between the sacral and the profane becomes the border between the spectacle and the public. The institutions staging the spectacles of different kind – from sports events up to theatre performances – are the modern institutions of care that prevent the sacred from its total disappearance in the profane society of work. Now, the traditional festival involved the whole population – if not of the world then at least one of its regions. That is why the traditional festivals as well as early Christian festivities did not have a character of competition. And participation in these festivals and festivities did not require excessive, superhuman, creative efforts. However, in the secular age, festivals and carnivals became spectacles and tourist attractions. The Christian mass has also become a show. Earlier, it was God and gods who took the position of the spectators and judges of human affairs. Today the role of spectatorship has become secularized. The public has replaced God and become the big Other of the spectacle. And it is precisely the gaze of the other, or the gaze of the public, that mobilizes the bodies of the actors. God could see into souls. The public can see and judge only bodies, their movements and their actions. However, the public is supposed to be always right. Of course, the individuals which compose the public have their own professions, ordinary lives and everyday problems. But at the moment at which they take the position of pure contemplation, they turn into a public – its gaze becomes divine: *vox populi* becomes *vox dei*.

It is not the explosion of vital forces but the gaze of the other, of God, of the public, that compels the actors to invest additional effort and work. We compete for attention, success, fame and money. The philosophers also compete for the favour of the divinized public. This competition takes place inside the institutions – inside academia for philosophers, but also in art, and sport. These institutions present themselves as guardians of truth or taste or scientific correctness. But they depend on fundraising that in turn depends on the public interest in and support for this or that idea, art exhibition or sports event. In all these spheres, as Kojève rightly noted, success is dependent on the recognition by the nonprofessional, non-knowing public. Sociologists and PR people try to explain the logic and dynamics of public preferences. The problem is that all these explanations are also competitive and must be accepted by the public to be recognized as true. Thus, the divine gaze of the public remains transcendent, as was the gaze of God. At the same time, one cannot assume that the public loves the spectacles of philosophy, art or science. The public is, rather, similar to *la dame sans merci* of the medieval *minnesingers* – she does not care about the loser but she also does not care so much about the winner because she knows that he will lose the next time.

The Nietzschean and post-Nietzschean celebration of vital forces and creativity was a reaction to standard bourgeois 'reasonable' behaviour neglecting art, poetry and music as an unreasonable waste of energy and time. The humans were recognized not only as the agents of rational economy and politics but also as bodies driven by 'irrational' desires, vital forces and the will to power. These forces are universal, they integrate the individual human being into the whole of the Universe, including the Sun and black holes. All kinds of irrational activities, such as art and poetry, are manifestations of these vital forces, which know nothing about human knowledge and ideas of the true and good. The vital forces, the will to power, are 'beyond good and evil'. The rationalistic and moralistic critique of art and poetry misses the point. This critique is always particular because it is dictated by specific cultural conventions of what is considered in a particular culture as being rational and moral, whereas the forces of creativity are eternal and universal – as eternal and universal as the Universe itself. The ideology of creativity was readily accepted by artistic circles because it looked like a justification of the artistic freedom to break any rationalistic and moralistic conventions. But this ideology was also accepted by bourgeois society as a whole because it soon enough morphed into the ideology of consumption. Indeed, from the rational point of view, consumption is an unproductive waste of energy. But it can be easily legitimized as the satisfaction of human bodies' needs, drives and desires. And the capitalist economy needs consumption as well as production, because if products are not consumed it makes no economic sense to produce them.

However, if the ideology of creativity is the justification of art and culture it is to the same degree the justification for their destruction. For this ideology, a particular artwork is not relevant – what is relevant is the creativity that produced it. A particular artist is also irrelevant: if that artist dies, the forces of creativity will find another embodiment for artistic activity. In fact, the whole of humanity becomes irrelevant because needs, drives and desires operate also in animals and plants and maybe also in inorganic matter (see, for example, the forces of gravitation). The spectacle of culture, be it a piece of theatre or a sporting event, always offers the same spectacle of the will to power – of the effort to win a competition. Who is a winner or loser is actually irrelevant. Tomorrow, they will be different, but the spectacle will not change. The effect is the same as in a case of the Platonic cave: everybody who leaves the cave sees the same light.

Now let us imagine that the philosopher, instead of returning to the cave, remains at its entrance. In this way, he or she is able to look at the people who are moving from one end to the other carrying different objects – shadows of which are seen on the walls of the cave. Thus, the philosopher moves from the position of contemplation of the eternal light to the position of art critic. Now, he or she can analyse which objects are more interesting and stimulating and which are not, who is moving and placing these objects in an interesting manner and who is not. If we assume that the spectacle of this movement is eternal, the position of the art critic also becomes eternal – even if art itself is changing all the time. The world of reason and morality seemed to Plato to be eternal. But the spectacle of creativity is also eternal – the eternal return of the same. As the spectator of this spectacle, the art critic joins the public, who do not necessarily look at the wall but are able to see everything that happens in the cave. They can also see the whole scene of dragging of the philosopher closer and closer towards the light and his or her return to the cave. This spectacle is offered by academia – and the spectator of this spectacle is, obviously, the same people, who remain in their usual places.

However, the spectacle survives only if its public survives. After all, it is only the people that have 'great health' and not an isolated individual. The only way for a philosopher to participate in this great health is to join the public. And it is precisely what Hegel and Nietzsche de facto do. In his *Phenomenology*, Hegel used the set of historical examples that was already familiar to his readers. Nietzsche believed that his books would be successful in the future because they could be easily inscribed in the evolution of the general public from Christian values towards the ideal of personal success. Kojève had it right: it is the desire of recognition by the public that inspires the spectacle of culture and politics. The supreme caretaker is the public. The modern spectacle takes place in front of the democratic public. Thus, the central question is this: Who is the demos? Or: Who is the people?

8

Who Is the People?

The question about the relationship between the spectacle and the people, or *Volk*, was raised by Richard Wagner in his treatise 'The Artwork of the Future', which he wrote in exile in Zürich after the suppression of the 1848 revolution in Germany. Wagner rejects the domination of the bourgeois public over the spectacle and its actors – the appreciating gaze of the connoisseurs that provokes competition among the artists. Instead, Wagner wants to address the ordinary people, the *Volk*. And thus he asks: '*Who is then the Volk?*—It is absolutely necessary that, before proceeding further, we should agree upon the answer to this weightiest of questions.' And he answers this question in the following way: 'The "*Volk*" is the epitome of all those men *who feel a common and collective Want* (*gemeinschaftliche Noth*)' And further: 'only the assuagement of a genuine Need is Necessity; and it is *the Volk alone that acts according to Necessity's behests*, and therefore irresistibly, victoriously, and right as none besides.'[1] Therefore, all those who do not feel the true, collective want but are guided by egoism and caprice do not belong to the *Volk* and are, in fact, its sworn enemies. Caprice stands under the dictatorship of fashion and produces the artificial need for luxury that, unfortunately, involves also art:

> The soul of Fashion is the most absolute uniformity, and its god an egoistic, sexless, barren god. Its motive force is therefore arbitrary alteration, unnecessary change, confused and restless striving after the opposite of its essential uniformity. Its might is the might of habit. But *Habit* is the invincible despot that rules all weaklings, cowards, and those bereft of veritable need. Habit is the communism

1 Richard Wagner, *The Artwork of the Future*, in *Richard Wagner's Prose Works*, vol. 1, trans. William Ashton Ellis, London: Kegan Paul, 1895, p. 75. (Wagner's italics in the original)

> of egoism, the tough, unyielding swathe of mutual, free-from-want self-interest; its artificial life-pulse is even that of Fashion.[2]

Now Wagner opposes to the art of his time dominated by fashion his own project of the universal artwork (*Gesamtkunstwerk*) that will unite the whole *Volk* and inaugurate true communism, instead of the false communism of habit.

Here, Wagner argues as a true revolutionary. He does not accept the bourgeois public of his time as part of the *Volk*. Instead, he proclaims only the poor and oppressed to be the true *Volk* – the true public of his theatre. Of course, he knows that, under the dominant economic and cultural conditions of his time, the poor cannot become his public. Wagner's audience has to remain an imaginary audience – at least until the coming revolution. But this orientation towards the imaginary, future, coming audience allowed Wagner to ignore his actual bourgeois audience and its criteria of competition, excellence and fashion. Wagner believed that the art of the future would be collective communal art. And he believed that the artists would be also members of a coming community. The artists would not only perform for an audience – they would represent this audience on the stage. The individual would become one of many – and not a winner in a specialized, professionalized competition.

Indeed, Wagner argues that only through death can the individual demonstrate the rejection of caprice and fashion:

> The last, completest renunciation (*Entäusserung*) of his personal egoism, the demonstration of his full ascension into universalism, a man can only show us by his *Death*; and that not by his accidental, but by his *necessary* death, the logical sequel to his actions, the last fulfilment of his being.
>
> *The celebration of such a Death is the noblest thing that men can enter on*. It reveals to us in the nature of this one man, laid bare by death, the whole content of universal human nature.[3]

---

2 Ibid., p. 84.
3 Ibid., p. 199.

The universal artwork as spectacle should be produced by a free artistic association. For the production of a particular spectacle, this association should be subjected to the will of the poet and, at the same time, the actor who plays the main hero. This actor functions as a temporary lawgiver and even dictator – until the spectacle is finished and his hero dies. Then the association selects a new actor to play the death of the next hero, and so on. Here, death becomes a spectacle for the living. Thus, time and again, the spectacle confirms the immortality of the public as audience – the heroes come and go but the audience remains. The spectacle is temporary, but the lifetime of its audience is undetermined and potentially eternal. Wagner treated the audience as the decisive factor of every spectacle. Not the creators – the artists, writers or actors – but the public are the real bearers of the spectacle and, in general, of art. Art is always made for the spectators, listeners and readers and so anticipates their reactions. The real driving force of any cultural activity is not the health and energy of the authors but the assumed health of the audience. The real crisis begins when this assumption becomes doubtful.

At the beginning of his treatise, Wagner states that mankind presents itself as divided into nations. Of course, Wagner proclaims his universal artwork to be a way to unite the whole of mankind. However, the transformation of the egoist into the communist can be also understood as his ascension into a national community. Wagner opposes the *Volk* that experiences existential need to the cosmopolitan bourgeois public that feels no real need and does not belong to any particular ethnic community. Initially, Wagner saw Greek culture as a model for a universal culture. At the time of the 1848 revolution, ancient Greek art was still considered to be a universal ideal. Marx also shared this aesthetic appreciation of Greek antiquity. However, Wagner later became more and more interested in old Germanic mythology. The community was now understood as an ethnic community and not the community of the poor.

According to Nietzsche's interpretation of the 'case of Wagner', that is precisely the reason for the degradation of Wagnerianism. Nietzsche starts by reminding the reader that Wagner was originally a revolutionary:

> Half his lifetime Wagner believed in the *Revolution* as only a Frenchman could have believed in it. He sought it in the runic inscriptions of myths, he thought he had found a typical revolutionary in Siegfried.—'Whence arises all the evil in this world?' Wagner asked himself. From 'old contracts', he replied, as all revolutionary ideologists have done. In plain English: from customs, laws, morals, institutions, from all those things upon which the ancient world and ancient society rests. 'How can one get rid of the evil in this world? How can one get rid of ancient society?' Only by declaring war against 'contracts' (traditions, morality). *This Siegfried does.*[4]

However, to Nietzsche, the audience of Wagner's *Bayreuther Festspiele* did not look healthy, revolutionary and optimistic. On the contrary, this audience was a collection of typical representatives of the decadent European bourgeoisie of that time: 'German youths, horned Siegfrieds and other Wagnerites, require the sublime, the profound, and the overwhelming.'[5] As a result, Wagner began to produce the decadent, sick, false spectacle – the art that his public expected from him. The decadent audience infected the creator, the author, and made him produce decadent art. The way in which Wagner has chosen his *Volk* became fateful. The case of Wagner shows that even the great creator cannot transcend the society of care. Even if this creator imitates the festivals of sacred, mythical time, as Wagner did, he remains in the framework of the institutions of care – one of which is the modern theatre – and becomes confronted by the 'decadent' public that is domesticated by the biopolitical state. However, it is precisely this public that supports the cultural institutions instead of destroying them and shows itself as ready to attend the performances of Wagner's operas and read Nietzsche's books. After all, the case of Wagner is also the case of Nietzsche.

4 *Complete Works of Friedrich Nietzsche*, ed. Oscar Levy, trans. Anthony M. Ludovici, vol. 8, *The Case of Wagner*, New York: Macmillan, 1911, pp. 9–10.
5 Ibid., p.15.

9

Care as Being of the *Dasein*

For the first time in the history of philosophy, the notion of care took central place in Heidegger's *Being and Time*. And one can even argue that the conflict between self-care – understood as self-assertion – and the institutions of modern, public care is at the centre of Heidegger's philosophical discourse. Heidegger follows his teacher Edmund Husserl by rejecting the 'natural attitude' that understands human beings as animals among other animals, things among other things. Man is not primarily a living organism moved by vital needs and drives – similar to other organisms like animals or plants. Heidegger defines man as *Dasein* (being-there) – as being-in-the-world. Here, being in the world means the impossibility to think *Dasein* as a 'subject' opposed to the world as an 'object'. The world is correlative to the *Dasein* – they cannot be separated from each other. The *Dasein* knows that its existence is endangered by death, that its world can disappear – so *Dasein* has the angst of death. The existence of *Dasein* is a project directed towards the future – we permanently plan something for the future. This planning presupposes that we further exist – and have to care about our existence. Our relationship to our world has the character of care (*Sorge*) and, actually, of self-care. Self-care is the fundamental mode of being of the *Dasein*.[1]

In German, the word *Sorge* (care) has at least two different but interconnected meanings. *Sich über etwas Sorgen machen* means to be worried about something. *Dasein* is worried about the existence of its world because its world can disappear. *Fuer etwas Sorge tragen* means to care about something. When I am worried about my existence I also care about it. That is why the being of *Dasein* is defined as care. *Dasein* is there because it cares for itself – and it is there in the

1 Martin Heidegger, *Being and Time*, trans. John Macquarrie and Edward Robinson, Oxford: Blackwell, 1962, pp. 225ff.

mode of worrying about itself. Here, care becomes the central ontological mode of human existence. In this context Heidegger cites an ancient Greek fable:

> Once when 'Care' was crossing a river, she saw some clay; she thoughtfully took up a piece and began to shape it. While she was meditating on what she had made, Jupiter came by. 'Care' asked him to give it spirit, and this he gladly granted. But when she wanted her name to be bestowed upon it, he forbade this, and demanded that it be given his name instead. While 'Care' and Jupiter were disputing, Earth arose and desired that her own name be conferred on the creature, since she had furnished it with part of her body. They asked Saturn to be their arbiter, and he made the following decision, which seemed a just one: 'Since you, Jupiter, have given its spirit, you shall receive that spirit at its death; and since you, Earth, have given its body, you shall receive its body. But since "Care" first shaped this creature, she shall possess it as long as it lives. And because there is now a dispute among you as to its name, let it be called "*homo*," for it is made out of *humus* (earth).'[2]

In later texts by Heidegger, the notion of care disappears almost completely. This disappearance is central for understanding these texts – and for understanding Heidegger's intellectual trajectory in general. Care is understood by Heidegger as care about the world of *Dasein*: 'In each case Dasein is its possibility, and it "has" this possibility, but not just as a property [*eigenschaftlich*], as something present-at-hand would. And because *Dasein* is in each case essentially its own possibility, it can, in its very Being, "choose" itself and win itself; it can also lose itself and never win itself; or only "seem" to do so.'[3] *Dasein* loses itself when it forgets its chosen mode of existing, when it begins to understand itself as a thing in the world and not as existing in-the-world. Self-care presupposes a fight for the specific mode of existence

2 Ibid., p. 242.
3 Ibid., p. 68.

of a *Dasein* in-the-world and against becoming a thing in the world controlled by the other or others.

That does not mean that *Dasein* is sovereign and rules its world. *Dasein* simply exists. The world originally belongs to *Dasein*, to its specific mode of existence. *Dasein* is in the world but not in control of the world. The danger appears and grows precisely when *Dasein* tries to control its world by technological means, to become a subject that dominates its world reduced to the object. Let us look at the example that Heidegger uses to illustrate this danger in his essay on technology:

> The hydroelectric plant is set into the current of the Rhine. It sets the Rhine to supplying its hydraulic pressure, which then sets the turbines turning. This turning sets those machines in motion whose thrust sets going the electric current for which the long-distance power station and its network of cables are set up to dispatch electricity ... In order that we may even remotely consider the monstrousness that reigns here, let us ponder for a moment the contrast that speaks out of the two titles, 'The Rhine' as dammed up into the power works, and 'The Rhine' as uttered out of the art work, in Hölderlin's hymn by that name.[4]

Indeed, Hölderlin's hymn celebrates the Rhine as part of the German world, whereas the power station uses the Rhine as a tool or, rather, as a resource. And Heidegger adds: 'But, it will be replied, the Rhine is still a river in the landscape, is it not? Perhaps. But how? In no other way than as an object on call for inspection by a tour group ordered there by the vacation industry.'[5] Now one can ask: what is so bad about the steady supply of electricity – and, for that matter, about organized tourism? The answer is: Here *Dasein* loses itself and becomes confronted with the danger to be also treated as a raw material for technological processing. And the example that Heidegger chooses to demonstrate such a

4 Martin Heidegger, *The Question Concerning Technology*, in *Basic Writings*, ed. David Farrell Krell, New York: Harper/Collins, 1973, p. 321.

5 Ibid., p. 323.

possibility is precisely the medical system: 'The current talk about human resources, about the supply of patients for a clinic, gives evidence of this.'[6] The medical care of human bodies kills their world, their authentic mode of being and turns them into raw material for the medical industry. Humans usually do not see this danger:

> The forester who, in the wood, measures the felled timber and to all appearances walks the same forest path in the same way so as did his grandfather is today commanded by profit-making in the lumber industry, whether he knows it or not. He is made subordinate to the orderability of cellulose, which for its part is challenged forth by the need for paper, which is then delivered to newspapers and illustrated magazines. The latter, in their turn, set public opinion to swallowing what is printed, so that a set configuration of opinion becomes available on demand.[7]

In other words, *Dasein* no longer exists in the mode of self-care and has therefore lost its original ontological status. Modern *Dasein* is imprisoned and controlled by technology. But Heidegger does not lose hope: 'Wherever man opens his eyes and ears, unlocks his heart, and gives himself over to meditating and striving, shaping and working, entreating and thanking, he finds himself everywhere already brought into the unconcealed.'[8] The problem is, however, that this unconcealment opens us up precisely to the process of forgetting of being in the middle of which we exist.

According to Heidegger, the unconcealment of being happens through art. However, right at the beginning of his essay 'The Origin of the Work of Art' (1935–6), Heidegger states that artworks are treated by our civilization as mere things:

> If we consider the works in their untouched reality and do not deceive ourselves, the result is that works are as naturally present as

6 Ibid.
7 Ibid.
8 Ibid., p. 324.

> are things. The picture hangs on the wall like a rifle or a hat . . . Works of art are shipped like coal from the Ruhr and logs from the Black Forest. During the First World War Hölderlin's hymns were packed in the soldier's knapsack together with cleaning gear. Beethoven's quartets lie in the storerooms of the publishing house like potatoes in a cellar. All works have this thingly character.[9]

Hölderlin's hymn thus actually shares the fate of Rhine itself. And Heidegger writes further that 'this crude and external view of the work is objectionable to us. Shippers or charwomen in museums may operate with such a conception of art. We, however, have to take works as they are encountered by those who experience and enjoy them.'[10] But why does Heidegger reject the perspective of shippers and charwomen? Here, again, the opposition between having a world and being a thing in the world plays the decisive role.

According to Heidegger, the artwork is the work of truth – and truth is the unconcealment of the world in which the artist lives. As an example Heidegger uses a painting by Van Gogh that shows a pair of shoes. Heidegger writes that these dirty, worn-out shoes reveal the world of a peasant woman who spent her life working hard on the land.[11] In fact, Van Gogh depicted his own shoes in this painting. But that is not the point here. For Heidegger, these shoes opened up the gaze to the world of peasant life in which both Van Gogh and Heidegger had also participated. Van Gogh went through the fields in a search for motifs for his paintings; Heidegger lived in a village.

However, artwork is not only a revelation of the world but also the object of an art business. For Heidegger, it means that the artwork is a place of conflict between World and Earth. The world opened up by the artist becomes closed in by the materiality, thingness of the work – by the return of this work to the earth out of which the work is made. Here, one can easily recognize the reference to the Greek fable from

9 Heidegger, *The Origin of the Work of Art*, in *Basic Writings*, p. 145.

10 Ibid.

11 Ibid., pp. 158ff.

Being and Time: the world of care disappears when *Dasein* dies – only a thing, a corpse, remains and becomes absorbed by earth. Here, the analogy between *Dasein* and the artwork becomes obvious. In the museum, one sees not the artworks but their dead bodies – not the worlds that the artworks reveal but these works as material, 'earthly' things that are taken care of by the 'art industry'. Here, the work experiences world-withdrawal and world-decay that cannot be undone.[12]

However, the world that was revealed through the work of art remains open if the 'people' (*das Volk*) still live in this world and care for it. Here again, as in Nietzsche's treatise on Wagner, the artwork is supposed to survive only if the people survive that serve as this work's authentic spectators because the mode of *Dasein* of this *Volk* coincides with the mode of *Dasein* of the artist. That is why the preservation of a particular artwork does not mean its mere conservation and restoration in a museum. Rather, it means preservation of the way of life that became unconcealed in this artwork. In this sense, creation and preservation of the artwork belong together. The work gives an impulse, a quantum of energy to its public, to the *Volk*, by revealing its world – and the mode of *Dasein* of the *Volk* remains the same as long as this impulse remains historically active. Even if Heidegger rejects the Nietzschean will to power as 'metaphysical' he still understands 'creative work' as produced by a surplus of energy. This is not the artist's own, individual energy but the influx (*Sprung*) of energy that is given by Being (*Ur-Sprung* means 'origin' in German) which the artist is able to absorb in the rare moments when the artist finds himself or herself in the 'clearing of being' (*Lichtung des Seins*). The artwork is able to transmit this energy to the historical *Volk* to which this artist belongs: 'That is because art is in its essence an origin, a distinctive way in which truth comes into being, that is, becomes historical'.[13] And it is precisely this distinctive way that one has to care for. The artist cares about the historical fate of his or her *Volk* – even if the artist cannot fully control it.

---

12 Ibid., p. 166.
13 Ibid., p. 202.

10

Under the Gaze of the Charwoman

We have learned the way the art lover sees art. But let us consider more closely the gaze of a charwoman. The charwoman left her original world in which she remained in direct contact with nature, with *phusis*, to become a worker in the system of technological care, maintenance and restoration of artworks as material objects. She no longer lives in the world that Van Gogh revealed. The painting of Van Gogh is for her just a piece of matter – of earth. But what then is the difference between the peasant woman and the charwoman? Both of them care for the earth. Indeed, the charwoman cares for the painting by Van Gogh in a way similar to the way in which the peasant woman cares for the field she cultivates. The charwoman sees this painting as a thing, a canvas covered by paint – in need of certain conditions of temperature, light, clean air and humidity. It is obvious that, for the charwoman, the museum is her world, one that she shares with the visitors who behave themselves according to the museum's rules – for example, those who do not come in with dirty shoes. So the question emerges: Why does the world of the charwoman deserve any less unconcealment through art than the world of the peasant woman? After all, the charwoman also exists and, thus, practises her *Dasein* in a mode of care concerned with artworks. Of course, one can say that her work of care is a part of an institution of care. She is not autonomous in her decisions concerning her care practice. But that does not mean that she has lost her *Dasein*. She has her own field of activity, and she is able to practise her work of care in a more or less responsible way. Can one say that the peasant woman, on the contrary, has complete autonomy of self-care? Obviously not, because she is a citizen, dependent on the market for selling her products and so on.

This means that, when we take care of a certain tradition and begin to practise it here and now with the goal of helping this tradition survive, our mode of care should change according to the way in which the world has changed. Thus, when we see that works of art are more and more produced for a museum, does this change mean that we have somehow 'betrayed' art and its mission? Not at all. Of course, we cannot only care for artworks from the past. To care for a tradition means to continue it – in this case, to produce new artworks. But what does it mean to continue an artistic tradition? Does it mean to cultivate the old artistic techniques? Or to produce the old life forms that produced these techniques in the first place? It seems that this kind of care work would be too exhausting for the caretakers – especially if they are confronted with art production on a greater scale. Thus, the question emerges: What are the minimal conditions for a work of art to be recognized as a work of art – and, as such, as a continuation of an art tradition that deserves the work of care?

That was the central question that the avant-garde tried to answer. One can argue that the art of the avant-garde was precisely the revelation of the world of the charwoman. Indeed, the artists of the avant-garde understood works of art as things that present themselves to the gaze of the spectator as they are and do not represent anything else. There is a widespread opinion that the art of the avant-garde was a manifestation of creativity – an explosion of the vital creative forces. In reality, however, this art was a result of reflection on and expansion of care. Thus, Albert Gleizes and Jean Metzinger state right at the beginning of their book on Cubism: 'A painting carries within itself its *raison d'être*. You may take it with impunity from a church to a drawing room, from a museum to a study.'[1] And, further, after stating that everything that is depicted on a painting is already removed from its natural environment and put into an exhibition space, they write: 'It [a painting] has just so much importance as a catalogue number, or a title at the bottom of a picture-frame. To contest this is to deny the space of painters; it is to deny painting.'[2] In other words, for Gleizes and Metzinger, a painting is first of all a mere thing circulating

1 Albert Gleizes and Jean Metzinger, *Cubism*, London: T. F. Unwin, 1913, p. 19. First published as *Du 'Cubism'*, Paris: Eugène Figuière et Cie., 1912.

2 Ibid., p. 26.

through the art system. And they see Cubism as asserting and explicitly manifesting this autonomous character of an individual painting as a material object that should not necessarily depict and represent any other object in the world. In other words, they join the bureaucratic, managerial definition of painting that is practised by the museum's or gallery's staff for whom a painting is a mere thing registered under a certain number – and then design their own paintings according to this definition.

The avant-garde reduced representation, narrative, everything figurative and naturalistic, to present artworks as mere things. The history of avant-garde movements is the history of these reductions – from the *Black Square* of Malevich to the 'unspecific objects' by Donald Judd. Since Duchamp, art care was expanded towards all possible things in everyday life. Artists began to take over the role of curators and organize exhibitions and publications. The word 'curator' comes, actually, from the same word, *cura*, or care. The curator takes care of the artworks with the goal of keeping them visible – accessible for contemplation. Of course, we tend to associate a curator with an exhibition maker who uses the artworks in an artificially created context. However, all the exhibitions are temporary – and, if an artwork is not accidentally damaged, it can be shown again in a different context. The same can be said about private and public collections and the art market in general. This is the basic difference between the artwork and the tool and between artworks and goods for consumption. During its time in use, a tool becomes worn out and consumption goods are used up, destroyed. Artworks, however, get a technical guarantee of permanence because they are there not for use and consumption but for contemplation alone. It remains, of course, an inescapable question why these particular things are functioning as objects of contemplation and not others. But, first of all, we can ask why should we contemplate any thing whatsoever?

It was the French Revolution that turned the things that were earlier used by the Church and the aristocracy as mere tools into artworks – that is, into objects that were exhibited in a museum, originally in the Louvre, only to be looked at. The secularism of the French

Revolution abolished the contemplation of God as the highest goal of life – and replaced it with the contemplation of 'beautiful' material objects. In other words, art was initially produced by revolutionary violence. During premodern history, a change of cultural regimes and conventions, including religions and political systems, led to radical iconoclastic acts, the physical destruction of the objects related to previous cultural forms and attitudes. The French Revolution offered a new way to deal with valuable things from the past: instead of being destroyed, they were defunctionalized and presented as art. It is this revolutionary transformation of the Louvre that Kant obviously has in mind when he writes in his *Critique of the Power of Judgment*:

> If someone asks me whether I find the palace that I see before me beautiful, I may well say that I do not like that sort of thing . . . in true *Rousseauesque* style I might even vilify the vanity of the great who waste the sweat of the people on such superfluous things . . . All of this might be conceded to me and approved; but that is not what is at issue here . . . One must not be in the least biased in favor of the existence of the thing, but must be entirely indifferent in this respect in order to play the judge in the matter of taste.[3]

The French Revolution introduced a new type of thing: defunctionalized tools understood as artworks and cared about by the curators.

It is often deplored that humans have become 'objectified' because objectification is associated with slavery. However, becoming a thing does not necessarily mean for a human being becoming a tool. Quite the contrary, becoming a thing can mean becoming an object of care. There is an obvious parallel between the hospital and the museum. Both have a goal of care and protection – of human bodies or things. Indeed, the protection of art objects can be compared to the medical protection of the human body. After all, the idea of protection of

3 Immanuel Kant, *Critique of the Power of Judgment*, ed. Paul Guyer, trans. Paul Guyer and Eric Matthews, Cambridge: Cambridge University Press, 2000, pp. 90–1.

human bodies through human rights was also introduced by the French Revolution. There is a close relationship between art and humanism. According to the principles of humanism, the human being can be only contemplated – but not actively used: killed, violated, enslaved. The humanist programme was summarized by Kant with a famous formulation: in the enlightened, secular society man is supposed to be never treated as a means but only as a goal. That is why we see slavery as barbaric. But to use an artwork in the same way as we use other things and commodities is also considered as barbaric. And what is most important here is that humans are defined by the secular gaze only as objects having a certain, human, form.

The human gaze does not see the human soul – that was the privilege of God. The human gaze sees only the human body. Our rights are related to the image that we offer to the gaze of others. That is why we are so much interested in this image. And that is also why we are interested in the protection of art and protection by art. Humans are protected only in so far as they are perceived by others as artworks produced by the greatest Artist – Nature itself. Not accidentally, in the nineteenth century – the century of humanism par excellence – the form of the human body was considered as the most beautiful among all the other forms, such as the forms of trees, fruits and waterfalls. And, of course, humans are well aware of their status as artworks – and try, time and again, to improve and stabilize this status. Human beings traditionally want to be desired, admired, looked at – to feel themselves as especially precious works of art.

This analogy between the human body and the artwork was radicalized by Nikolay Fedorov at the end of nineteenth century in his project of 'the common task'.[4] (It is a standard translation of the original Russian title *Obshchee delo* which is, actually, in its turn the literal translation of the Latin *res publica*). The common task of humanity consists for Fedorov in artificial resurrection of all the previous

4 Nikolay Fedorov, *What Was Man Created For? The Philosophy of the Common Task*, trans. Elisabeth Koutaissoff and Marilyn Minto, London: Honeyglen/L'Age d'Homme, 1990.

generations. As the starting point for realization of this project, Fedorov chooses the museum. He rightly states that the very existence of the museum contradicts the general utilitarian, pragmatic spirit of the nineteenth century.[5] Fedorov saw nineteenth-century technology as internally divided. In his view, modern technology served primarily fashion and war – that is, finite, mortal life. It is only in relation to this technology that one can speak of progress, because fashion changes constantly with time. It also divides human generations: every generation has its own technology and despises the technology of its parents. But technology also functions as art. Fedorov understands art not as a matter of taste or, generally, aesthetics. Rather, art is for Fedorov the technology of preservation and revival of the past. There is no progress in art. Art does not wait for a better society of the future – it immortalizes here and now. In doing so, however, art, as it is practised in a bourgeois society, does not usually work with things themselves but merely with the images of things. The preserving, redemptive, reviving task of art thus ultimately remains unfulfilled.

To fulfil its mission, the art museum should include humans. Indeed, because each human being is simply a body among other bodies, a thing among other things, humans can also be blessed with the museum's immortality. For Fedorov, immortality is not a paradise for human souls but a museum for living human bodies. Divine grace is replaced by curatorial decisions and the technology of museum preservation. All of the people who have ever lived must rise from the dead as artworks and be preserved in a universal museum that would be identical with the universe as a whole. The state must become the museum of its population. Just as the museum's administration is responsible not only for the general holdings of the museum's collection but also for the state of every given work of art, making certain that the individual artworks are subjected to conservation and restoration when they threaten to decay, the state

5 Nikolay Fedorov, *Museum, Its Meaning and Mission*, in Arseny Zhilyaev, ed. *Avant-Garde Museology: e-flux classics*, Minneapolis: University of Minnesota Press, 2015, pp. 60–170.

should bear responsibility for the resurrection and immortal life of every individual person. The state can no longer permit itself to allow individuals to die privately or the dead to rest peacefully in their graves. Death's limits must be overcome by the state. One could say that biopower must become total – and not merely partial, as described by Foucault.

According to the famous phrase of Michel Foucault, the modern state makes life and lets die, in contrast to the sovereign state of the older variety that made death and let live. The modern state is concerned with birth rates, death rates and providing its population with health care. But if the survival of the population is central to the state's goals, the 'natural' death of any given individual is passively accepted by the state and treated as a private matter of this individual. Characteristically, Foucault understood the space of the museum as an 'other space', a heterotopic space. He spoke of the museum as a place where time is accumulated – and that was precisely what distinguished the museum from the space of 'real life'. Fedorov, by contrast, sought to unite life space with museum space, to overcome their heterogeneity, which he saw as ideologically motivated rather than ontologically given. The overcoming of the boundaries between life and death is here not a matter of introducing art into life but is rather a radical museumification of life, of transposing the whole society into the heterotopic museum space. By means of this unification of life space and museum space, museum conservation becomes the technology of eternal life. Such a technology is, of course, no longer 'democratic': no one expects the artworks that are preserved in a museum collection to democratically elect the museum curator who will care for them. As soon as human beings become radically modern – that is, as soon as they come to be understood as bodies among other bodies, as things among other things – they have to accept that state-organized technology will treat them accordingly. This acceptance has a crucial precondition, however: the explicit goal for the new power must be eternal life here on earth for everyone. Only then does the state cease to be a partial, limited biopower of the sort described by Foucault and become a total biopower.

Heidegger assumes that, when the individual *Dasein* survives the loss of its world, it becomes a thing in the world of others. However, in our contemporary world, such a survival is not an exception but rather a rule. Indeed, our world is dominated by migration – people flee from wars and economic calamities. They leave their symbolic bodies behind and bring with them only the histories of their illnesses. In fact, their former cultures can also be seen as their former illnesses. But even if people remain at home, their world can disappear – being cancelled by technological progress, war or revolution. Heidegger's charwoman was probably a peasant woman before an economic crisis brought her to the city, where she found her new job. The first result of any technological or political revolution is the defunctionalization of many human bodies – analogous to the defunctionalization of artworks as a result of artistic revolutions.

In his *The Birth of the Clinic*, Foucault thematizes the early, still utopian version of this connection between revolution and health. He cites Sabarot de l'Avernière, a prolific author of the revolutionary epoch, who writes about the prerevolutionary rich:

> Living in the midst of ease, surrounded by the pleasures of life, their irascible pride, their bitter spleen, their abuses, and the excesses to which their contempt of all principles leads them makes them prey to infirmities of every kind; soon . . . their faces are furrowed, their hair turns white, and diseases harvest them before their time. Meanwhile, the poor, subjected to the despotism of the rich and of their kings, know only taxes that reduce them to penury, scarcity that benefits only the profiteers, and unhealthy housing that forces them 'either to refrain from raising families or to procreate weak, miserable creatures'.[6]

Here, the hard work of *Dasein* is understood as a result of exploitation of the poor by the rich. The revolution has the goal of liberating the human body from this exploitation and making it healthy:

---

6 Michel Foucault, *The Birth of the Clinic: An Archaeology of Medical Perception*, trans. A. M. Sheridan, London: Routledge, 1973, p. 33.

> And in a society that was free at last, in which inequalities were reduced, and in which concord reigned, the doctor would have no more than a temporary role: that of giving legislator and citizen advice as to the regulation of his heart and body. There would no longer be any need for academies and hospitals . . . And gradually, in this young city entirely dedicated to the happiness of possessing health, the face of the doctor would fade, leaving a faint trace in men's memories of a time of kings and wealth, in which they were impoverished, sick slaves.[7]

The revolution is understood here as the liberation of the human body from hard work. The society of work is replaced by the society of care – care by institutions and self-care.

One could say that, through the system of care, the human body becomes a readymade. It becomes defunctionalized, taken out of the context of previous occupations. In modern society, humans know themselves as working and/or fighting for prestige. But what happens with a body that – as a result of illness or age – has lost its capacity to work and fight? It becomes useless. It becomes a defunctionalized body of care. We know what awaits us after the end of our working days – not paradise but rather the hospital/museum. Our bodies that, during the biggest part of our lifetimes were used merely as working tools, become the precious objects of care. We tend to think that our value is measured by our usefulness to the society in which we live. But the system of care actually transcends the system of work. The system of care includes also the bodies that were never able to work and never will be. The universal system of medical care replaces the care of the upper classes of which Kojève was speaking just as the museum replaces the palace. Medicine does not serve all our desires but only the basic one – the desire for self-preservation. It is not a lot. But it demonstrates that our existence has more value than our work. To be healed is not the same as to be brought back to a usable state. However, if the system of care values the living body of the patient more than its economic use, what can be said about the value of care work?

7 Ibid., p. 34.

11

Work and Labour

In her book *The Human Condition*, Hannah Arendt argues that care work is traditionally less valued than productive work. Thus, in the ancient Greek tradition, care work was considered to be slave work because it had the body of the master as its object. Accordingly, Arendt draws a distinction between 'work', understood as the productive process, and 'labour', understood as the unproductive work of care, and writes: 'It is indeed the mark of all laboring that it leaves nothing behind, that the result of its effort is almost as quickly consumed as the effort is spent. And yet this effort, despite its futility, is born of a great urgency and motivated by a more powerful drive than anything else, because life itself depends upon it.'[1]

Further, Arendt argues that it was Marx who reversed the relationship between work and labour and subjected productive work to unproductive labour – labouring activity – by introducing the notion of 'labour power'. The labour of care is unproductive, but it produces 'labour power', which produces everything else. Humans possess 'productivity':

> This productivity does not lie in any of labor's products but in the human 'power', whose strength is not exhausted when it has produced the means of its own subsistence and survival but is capable of producing a 'surplus', that is, more than is necessary for its own 'reproduction'. It is because not labor itself but the surplus of human 'labor *power*' (*Arbeits*kraft) explains labor's productivity that Marx's introduction of this term, as Engels rightly remarked, constituted the most original and revolutionary element of his whole system.[2]

---

1 Hannah Arendt, *The Human Condition*, Chicago: University of Chicago Press, 1958, p. 87.

2 Ibid., p. 88.

Thus, all work becomes labour because 'all things would be understood, not in their worldly, objective quality, but as results of living labor power and functions of the life process.'[3] Arendt also sees so-called 'intellectual work' as a version of care work – caring not about living organisms but about big bureaucratic machines where care in a similar way does not leave any distinguishable traces. Obviously, for Arendt the figure of the modern intellectual is similar to the Kojevian figure of the Sage: the philosopher was creative but the Sage serves and cares.

This absence of the material, 'worldly' traces of human work irritates Arendt. Obviously, she experiences nostalgia for Nietzschean 'monumental history' of 'great men' (and women) who have built a transgenerational, transhistorical chain of solidarity and created the world in which we are still living. Indeed, when all work is understood as labour, the world becomes totally absorbed by life. Life is also a transhistorical process, but it is a collective, common process. This process is fluid. The individual emerges and disappears on the surface of this flow, but it cannot be historically stabilized. Here, the Heideggerian 'loss of the world' surfaces again. When *Dasein* practises self-care, it cares for its world. When *Dasein* becomes life, some other takes care of it. But how does *Dasein* become life? Arendt speaks about the pain that makes us forget the world around us and continues:

> The only activity which corresponds strictly to the experience of worldlessness, or rather to the loss of world that occurs in pain, is laboring, where the human body, its activity notwithstanding, is also thrown back upon itself, concentrates upon nothing but its own being alive, and remains imprisoned in its metabolism with nature without ever transcending or freeing itself from the recurring cycle of its own functioning.[4]

---

3 Ibid., p. 89.
4 Ibid., p. 115.

Life reveals itself in pain. When Marx, as Arendt suggests, saw human history as humanity's metabolism with nature, it means nothing else than that Marx saw humanity in pain.

As we have already seen, not only human bodies but the things of the world also need the labour of care that protects and maintains them. And Arendt herself explains well enough why this work may and even must fail. She introduces the notion of 'natality'. This notion means that 'every new generation can undo what has been done'.[5] One cannot preserve anything beyond one's lifetime. And this means precisely that everything is absorbed by the care involved in life's metabolism with nature. Towards the end of the book Arendt writes that life has become the only goal of men – and not an individual life but the life of the 'socialized man'. Arendt again renders Marx responsible for this shift in the understanding of life but, at the same time proclaims the victory of man as *animal laborans* to be historically inevitable – even if deplorable.[6]

Socialized man, or, rather, the socialized human body, is, according to Arendt, the most important historic result of the struggle between the society of private property and the labour movement. The primary form of private property is the privacy of the human body: the development of private property can be seen as an expansion of privacy through the process of appropriation by the human body of its environment. Arendt underlines the fact that, even in socialist societies, the physiological functions of the body remain private. She writes: 'In this aspect, the body becomes indeed the quintessence of all property because it is the only thing one could not share even if one wanted to. Nothing, in fact, is less common and less communicable, and therefore more securely shielded against the visibility and audibility of the public realm, than what goes on within the confines of the body.'[7] However, the emergence of the public and private institutions of care and, parallel to that, the rise of the labour

5 Ibid., p. 243.
6 Ibid., pp. 321ff.
7 Ibid., p. 112.

movement, which includes care workers, leads to the loss of privacy. My own body does not any longer belong to me. Its physiological functions, including its reproductive functions, become the subject of political discussions and bureaucratic procedures. Everybody lives in the anticipation of pain – and that means in anticipation of the loss of one's world and socialization as an object of care. That explains why, today, privacy has lost its protected status to a degree that Arendt would not be able to imagine.

The system of care is a medium through which the metabolism of the socialized body with nature takes place. This body is both physical and political at the same time. Its most intimate functions are institutionally accessible and become the topics of public discussion. This is not a new situation. In feudal society, in which power was inherited through the right of birth, the body of the master was the source of political legitimacy. That is why the care of his body had the highest political priority. In bourgeois society, the body lost its political relevance and became a mere tool used for social activity or work. As a result, bodies began to be separated from each other by their symbolic status. The experience of intimacy could be achieved only in sex and war – that means in situations of exception from the dominating symbolic order. For the system of care, on the contrary, all bodies are intimate and political at the same time. Here, the intimate and the political, the physical body and symbolic body, become identical.

This new identity of the intimate and the public is well illustrated in contemporary social media. Social networks like Facebook or Instagram offer to the global population an opportunity to post their most intimate photos, videos and texts and make them accessible to everyone – and internet users have no scruples about making use of them. In the era of the classical mass cultural spectacle, Andy Warhol famously predicted the fifteen minutes of fame during which an individual had a chance to get the attention of the media. But Warhol also produced films like *Sleep* which showed a man sleeping for several hours. Here the private becomes public. It was truly a beginning of the new age in which we still live. Through the internet, our symbolic bodies began more and more to coincide with our physical bodies. As more and more people use the internet to satisfy their most private needs and desires, these needs and desires become more and more publicly accessible. Today, accounts in social networks serve as primary versions of symbolic bodies – functioning as almost immediate extensions of the physical bodies of the users. The internet is passive – it only reacts to our desires, our questions, our clicks. But the internet is not only a mirror but also a camera that produces an image of our desiring self. And the content of the accounts does mostly refer to the ordinary, everyday life, which as such is totally uninteresting. If the ideology of creativity required an individual to present itself as different, unusual, even extraordinary, contemporary ideology requires self-presentation as merely another human person. It is obviously the best self-protective strategy in a very heterogeneous society that can become potentially dangerous for everyone at any moment. At the beginning of the internet era, there was a strange confidence in this new network tool. This confidence has over time been totally lost – not only because of the widespread knowledge of internet surveillance but also the use of the net as a medium for spreading all kinds of hate. In this sense, self-intimization serves primarily the goal of self-protection. But that means also that our private, personal bodies have become symbolic. Life has abandoned them – symbolic bodies cannot experience pain. Narcissistic self-exposure functions here as anaesthesia. The socialization and politicization of one's body seem to prevent the experience of its pain as 'my' pain – even before the intervention of any medical treatment. Here, the revelation of one's own body functions as mimicry.

In his book about mimicry, Caillois argues against the widespread impression that mimicry is the ability of the organism to become visually integrated in its surroundings.[8] Indeed, mimicry is usually associated with conformism – with the protective desire to become average, to look and act like everybody else. Caillois wanted to prove that there were, so to say, nonconformist forms of mimicry. He showed that some insects present themselves as bigger and more

8 Roger Caillois, *Méduse et Cie*, Paris: Gallimard, 1960.

dangerous than they actually are – with the goal of frightening possible aggressors.[9] One can read this book as a parody of the surrealist movement, the members of which tried to present themselves as more dangerous than they actually were, but in fact Caillois presents here a much more general theory of creativity as self-protection and self-care. Creativity is not an eruption of internal energy and the will to power but rather a skilful imitation of such an eruption that protects the weak physical body that is hidden behind it. This theory can be applied to Nietzsche, but not only to him. In his theory of the gaze, Lacan used this book by Caillois to make the point that art, and especially painting, is always a way not to expose but to protect the artist from exposure to the gaze of the other. As Lacan says, the gaze of the other is always an evil gaze. By producing artworks, artists try to redirect the gaze of the other from their own bodies to the body of their work – and thus to disarm the evil, harmful gaze of the spectator. Here creativity is understood not as an effect of the surplus of energy that imposes the artistic will on the world but as a defence of the weak against the aggression of the other. The revelation of their own private, intimate body and its needs and desires is the most economical way to create a protective symbolic body that can withstand the evil gaze of the other.

Our culture is often described as being narcissistic. And narcissism is understood as total concentration on oneself, as a lack of interest in society. However, it would be wrong to say that the mythological Narcissus was asocial. He was enchanted by the reflection of his body in the lake as an 'objective', profane image – produced by Nature itself and potentially accessible to everyone. And he assumed that others would also be fascinated by his worldly image. As part of Greek culture, he knew that he shared the aesthetic taste of other Greeks. However, contemporary humans cannot rely on the looks they were born with: they must practise self-design, and produce their own image with the goal of becoming liked across the extremely heterogeneous society in which we live. Even those

9 Ibid.

whose activities are limited to taking selfies still actively distribute them to get the 'likes' they want. None are as interested in the survival and well-being of society as the contemporary Narcissuses.

This interest is characteristically modern, secular, atheistic. Earlier, the desire for recognition and admiration by others, by society, was regarded as a sin because it substituted 'worldly' recognition for the only true spiritual recognition – external values for inner values. The primary relationship of the subject to society was religious, ethical. In the secular age, God was replaced by society, and instead of an ethical relationship, our relationship to society thus became erotic. To survive, the individual has to be liked. And to be liked it has to make itself likeable. Where religion once was, design emerged. As a result, design has transformed society itself into an exhibition space in which individuals appear as both artists and self-produced works of art. Self-design is a form of self-protection, self-care – and thus escapes Kant's famous distinction between disinterested aesthetic contemplation and the use of things guided by interests. The subject of self-design clearly has a vital interest in the image it offers to the outside world. And the decision of the spectator to like, or not to like, this image has grave personal and political consequences. That is why the subject of self-design is not only interested in its own image but also in the existence of the spectators of this image. Just as a lover is interested in the existence of a partner to be loved by, the subject of self-design is interested in the existence and structure of society to find recognition and receive admiration. The narcissistic desire for recognition strengthens the existing symbolic order of the society because it is these structures towards which this desire is directed. Here, the human body becomes an artwork – analogous to a museum item. One wants to be liked, to be cared about.

12

Revolutionary Care

But how is it possible to escape the necessity of self-presentation, of creation of a protective image, of self-design? This is the actual problem with which every revolutionary theory is confronted. One can argue that Alexander Bogdanov offered the clearest description of this problem in his *Tektology*. He described the revolutionary process using the notions of *egression* and *degression*. Egressive are all the traditional, centralized, authoritarian forms of social organization. He writes: 'Their forms have been quite varied in the history of mankind: patriarchal commune, feudal formation, slave-owning economy, the eastern despotism, bureaucracy, modem army, and petty bourgeois family, etc.'[1] All these forms of organization reveal themselves as unstable because, for any centralized power, it is difficult to control society in its smallest units. As a result, these units make themselves more or less independent and the egressive, authoritarian whole dissolves. That became especially obvious when the *ancien régime* began to be confronted with the Industrial Revolution:

> In machine production a new link of egression – a mechanism – is introduced between the hand of man and the working tool. Thus, a new broadening of egression is also achieved, and quite a significant one at that: the mechanism is free from the biological limitation of organs of the body and can control at the same time an indefinitely large number of instruments. Subsequently, the egression developed in a form of a chain of mechanisms, where some of them put into motion or regulated others.[2]

1 Alexander Bogdanov, *Essays in Tektology: The Universal Organization Science*, trans. George Gorelik, Seaside, CA: Intersystems Publications, 1980, p. 178.

2 Ibid., p. 185.

The chains of control become so long and difficult to manage that the egressive system of power dissolves. The post-egressive organization, in contrast, is based on the principle of plasticity:

> It denotes a mobile, flexible character of couplings of the complex, and ease in regrouping of its elements. It has a tremendous significance for organizational development. The more plastic is the complex, the greater is the number of combinations that can be formed under any conditions which change it, the richer is the material of selection, and the faster and more fully is its adaptation to these conditions.[3]

However, plasticity endangers living organisms because of the instability of their forms. As a reaction to this danger, the plastic organization becomes degresssive, or 'skeletal'. Bogdanov understands as skeletal all the forms of protection of the organism, including, for example, skin. One is reminded here of Caillois's book on the insects that have external skeletons that make them look dangerous through a kind of (anti)mimicry. Indeed, Bogdanov writes: 'Here belong clothing – an additional external skeleton of the body – and a dwelling, an analogous skeleton of a higher order; cases and boxes for the preservation of all kinds of products of labour, and vessels for liquids, etc.'[4] One could add hospitals and museums. What I call the symbolic body is also understood by Bogdanov as an external skeleton: '*Symbols* of various kinds, in particular the most typical and widespread of them – the word, represent an extraordinarily important and interesting case of degression.'[5] Indeed, Bogdanov understands language – together with all the rituals and conventions of its use – as a skeleton of the degressive society. Works of art also belong to this skeleton. Bogdanov very early saw their primarily protective function.

---

3 Ibid.
4 Ibid., p. 188.
5 Ibid., p. 189.

Thus Bogdanov writes: 'The point is exactly in this stability: symbols *fix*, i.e., fasten, hold and protect from decay the living plastic tissue of mental images, completely analogously to how the skeleton fixes the living, plastic tissue of the colloidal proteins of our body.'[6] The most skeletal and ossified societal form is the system of education that, paradoxically, tends to destroy the protective character of the individual human skeleton: 'So, for example, the child is told not be secretive, or that he should never tell a lie. This is convenient for educators; but in contemporary reality a man is doomed to perish if he is unable to hide his feelings and thoughts.'[7] Referring to Marx, Bogdanov further writes that the technical skeleton defines the economic and ideological skeleton of a society: 'Here the *primary* processes of selection and adaptation go on, on which subsequent changes in the course of the life of society depend: the initial point of social development or its bases turn out to be technical forms.'[8] It is very interesting that Heidegger also introduces the word *Gestell* (German for 'skeleton') as central to his theory of technology. *Gestell* also means 'apparatus'. Heidegger argues that the techno-social apparatus frames our view of the world. But we overlook the *Gestell* precisely because it directs and frames our gaze.[9]

Bogdanov's analysis explains why in a 'democratised' society all the projects aimed at further democratization, horizontality and plasticity lead nowhere. These projects are directed against authoritarianism and 'egressive' powers in the hope that all the vestiges of these authoritarian powers can be removed and a perfectly flat, horizontal, 'rhizomatic' society will become the society of freedom. But Bogdanov shows that horizontal societies still have to use language and other rituals of mutual understanding. Thus, individuals remain included in the degressive system of rules, rights and duties that build their own as well as the social skeleton. And society is still based on the presupposition that the bodies of its

6 Ibid.
7 Ibid., p. 198.
8 Ibid., p. 205.
9 Heidegger, 'The Question Concerning Technology', in *Basic Writings*, pp. 325ff.

members coincide with their external skeleton – in other words, that these members do not lie and cheat. That means that struggles for horizontality fail to reach their actual goal. Democratized societies are controlled not by authoritarian powers but by their skeleton, their *Gestell* – the rules of communication, the mode of decision making, the common language, the common mode of life, the technology that these societies use. When one requires even further democratization and horizontality, one makes procedural rules, the technology of common life, even more important, and thus the societal skeleton becomes even more inflexible and ossified.

That is why Bogdanov believes that only a highly centralized and truly egressive movement can break the conservative skeleton of democratic society and become truly emancipatory. Through such egressive movements, individuals and social groups break out from the protective skeleton and begin to control themselves and their environment. According to Bogdanov, only a religious cult or a political party can become such a disruptive, transformative force because both of them are egressive, centralized. The religious cult, however, necessarily appeals to the already existing skeletal forms of tradition and rituals – a religion can never be truly new. Ideology is for Bogdanov also degressive. So the true revolutionary, egressive party cannot be based on an inflexible ideology. In this respect, Bogdanov's description of egression reminds one of Georges Sorel's *Essay on Violence*.[10] Sorel stresses that Marx was not a utopian thinker and reacted ironically to all projects for designing the future. The revolution is truly revolutionary only when it opens an unforeseeable future. But the revolution is also not a result of the creative investment of additional energy but rather the decision not to support the existing order, not to care for it any more. The revolution requires not more, but less, energy than everyday, 'degressive' work. Sorel defines the general strike as the most radical form of revolutionary violence. It is not the violence that imposes a new law (as in the case of the French

10 Georges Sorel, *Reflections on Violence*, Cambridge: Cambridge University Press, 1999 [1912], pp. 72–3.

Revolution) but, on the contrary, the subversive violence that lets the old order collapse and opens up the space for a new order to emerge. The revolution has to produce a feeling of relief – not of a new obligation.

Bogdanov also believed that the revolutionary party should not use any already existing skeletal forms. It could be effective and succeed only if it became radically centralized. Bogdanov shows the perils of decentralization for such a party with an example taken from the history of the Russian Social-Democratic Workers' Party. That does not mean that Bogdanov expected that the Bolshevik Party would be forever egressive and disruptive. Rather, he believed that a period of degression and ossification will necessarily come after the establishment of a new egressive regime. The forces of egression and degression are involved in an eternal conflict. At every particular moment, one can choose between them, but one cannot completely escape being defined by both of them.[11]

The conflict between egression and degression can be understood as the conflict between self-care and care. Degressive, skeletal systems are systems of protection, of care. They are organized according to technological, economic and administrative rules and constraints that define the skeleton of the society. The patient should follow the dominant conventions: search for the appropriate health insurance, go to a physician located nearby or recommended by friends and acquaintances, and so on. However, the patient – or, rather, the patients – can use their relatively external, eccentric position towards the degressive medical system to start an egressive movement that takes power over this system – and transforms it in the interest of the patients and their health. Here, self-care begins to dominate over care.

The problematic of medical care was not foreign to Bogdanov – he was a physician by academic training and his *Tektology* is full of biological examples and references. For some time, Bogdanov was, besides Lenin, one of the leaders of the movement inside the Russian Social-Democratic Workers' Party that became the Bolshevik and

11 Bogdanov, *Essays in Tektology*, p. 183.

then Communist Party. By 1912, however, Bogdanov had abandoned revolutionary activity. He later became active in the post-revolutionary period as organizer of the famous *Proletkult*. The main idea of *Proletkult* was to motivate ordinary workers and peasants to make art. Everybody was accepted. There was almost no aesthetic censorship and selection. In a certain way, the *Proletkult* was a realization of Marx's idea of the deprofessionalization of art – its liberation from control by the art market. Art should become the direct manifestation of the proletarian desire for self-design – beyond questions of quality, usefulness and other criteria. Thus, it is quite understandable that the *Proletkult* was practically abolished by the Communist leadership in 1920 – according to the tektological principle of the centralization of egressive movements.

After the dissolution of the *Proletkult*, Bogdanov organized the Institute of Haematology and Blood Transfusion (1924–8). Bogdanov believed that blood transfusions between representatives of the older and younger generations would lead to the rejuvenation of the old one. According to some reports, the early results were very promising.[12] In 1928, Bogdanov exchanged his own blood with the blood of a female student who was ill with tuberculosis and malaria. As a result of this blood transfusion, Bogdanov died – and the student fully recovered.

Bogdanov's experiments with blood transfusion fit in with the post-revolutionary tendency to combine the Communist promise to build on Earth a happy life for all and the Fedorovian promise to realize immortality and resurrection by technological means. This tendency was shared by a wide range of party intellectuals from Lunacharsky to Trotsky. It was most clearly formulated in the manifesto of the group of what were called cosmist-immortalists: human rights should include the right to become immortal, regular rejuvenation, and free, individual travel in cosmic space.[13] As the

12 Alexander Bogdanov, 'Tektology of the Struggle against Old Age', in *Russian Cosmism*, ed. Boris Groys, Cambridge, MA: MIT Press, 2018, pp. 203ff.

13 See Alexander Svyatogor, 'Our Affirmations', in *Russian Cosmism*, ed. Groys, pp. 59–62.

functioning of the Institute of Haematology and Blood Transfusion shows, Bogdanov shared this egressive tendency of the biocosmist movement – egressive because its goals were realizable only under conditions of central planning and administration. But at the same time Bogdanov also had certain premonitions of the degressive ossification of this movement if it should become successful.

These premonitions are thematized in a short story under the title 'Immortality Day' that he published in 1912.[14] The scientist Fride, who a thousand years previously had discovered the method of making humans immortal, is to be celebrated on the anniversary of this discovery. During these thousand years, Fride had explored different sciences and arts – and had succeeded in all of them. But now he has lost his early enthusiasm and his relationship with his wife, which has lasted several centuries, has become a burden. Human life has become eternal, but the number of possible human thoughts and their combinations, as well as the number of possible natural events and their combinations, remains limited. For Nietzsche, the limited number of possible events in the finite, material world was proof that worldly existence is subject to the law of the eternal return of the same.[15] Walter Benjamin saw in this Nietzschean figure an attempt to guarantee individual happiness in the middle of a culture controlled by the ideology of progress – a culture in which the individual had to wait and wait until the promise of happiness would be fulfilled by collective effort.[16] But what was a hope for a mortal human being has become a curse for an immortal one. The eternal return of the same became a degressive form of immortality. However, under total biopolitical control the only possible egressive movement is the movement back towards human mortality. Fride decides to commit suicide and writes in his will: 'After one thousand years of my

14 Alexander Bogdanov, 'Immortality Day', in *Russian Cosmism*, ed. Groys, pp. 215ff.

15 Friedrich Nietzsche, *Gesammelte Werke*, Munich: München Musarion Verlag, 1926, vol. 19, p. 373.

16 Walter Benjamin, *Gesammelte Schriften*, Frankfurt am Main: Suhrkamp, 1982, Band V-1, p. 173.

existence I have come to the conclusion that life on Earth is a cycle of repetitions, especially intolerable for a man of genius, whose entire being yearns for innovation. This is one of nature's antinomies. I resolve it with suicide.'[17]

As a method of committing suicide, Fride choses to be burned at the stake because he thinks that this method is the most painful:

> At midnight the explosion of fireworks marked the arrival of the second millennium of human immortality. Fride pressed an electronic button which lit the fuse, and the pyre went up in flames. Terrible pain, of which he had some vague childhood recollection, disfigured his face. He frantically struggled to pull himself free, and an inhuman scream resounded in the alcove. But the iron chains held him firmly. Tongues of fire twisted around his body, hissing: 'Everything repeats itself!'[18]

Fride wants not merely to live but to feel himself truly alive. And, as Arendt rightly says, one can discover oneself as truly alive only in pain – so that it seems that the experience of extreme pain offers an escape from the anaesthetized, machine-like mode of existence imposed on men of the future by the institutional care that makes them healthy, immortal and forever bored. However, the act of self-immolation follows a well-established cultural pattern and, thus, does not lead Fride away from the prison of degressive repetitions. Burning at the stake was, indeed, practised over a long period of history – from the burning of medieval witches to the burning of Giordano Bruno. And here one should say that Bogdanov himself lost his life in a truly egressive manner – trying to heal a younger life by giving up an older one.

---

17 Bogdanov, 'Immortality Day', in *Russian Cosmism*, p. 225.

18 Ibid., p. 226.

Index